Gastric Ban for Rapid Weight Loss

Avoid the Risk of Gastric Band Surgery, Burn Fat, and Get Rid of a Food Addiction and Emotional Eating with Affirmations, Meditations, and Self-Hypnosis

Mia Rowse

© Copyright 2022 – Mia Rowse - All rights reserved.

The content contained within this book may not be reproduced, duplicated, or transmitted without direct written permission from the author or the publisher.
Under no circumstances will any blame or legal responsibility be held against the publisher, or author, for any damages, reparation, or monetary loss due to the information contained within this book, either directly or indirectly.

Legal Notice:
This book is copyright protected. It is only for personal use. You cannot amend, distribute, sell, use, quote or paraphrase any part, or the content within this book, without the consent of the author or publisher.

Disclaimer Notice:
Please note the information contained within this document is for educational and entertainment purposes only. All effort has been executed to present accurate, up to date, reliable, complete information. No warranties of any kind are declared or implied. Readers acknowledge that the author is not engaged in the rendering of legal, financial, medical or professional advice. The content within this book has been derived from various sources. Please consult a licensed professional before attempting any techniques outlined in this book.

This is a work of creative nonfiction. Some parts have been fictionalized in varying degrees, for various purposes.

By reading this document, the reader agrees that under no circumstances is the author responsible for any losses, direct or indirect, that are incurred as a result of the use of the information contained within this document, including, but not limited to, errors, omissions, or inaccuracies.

First Edition
First Edition: November 2022
This Paperback Edition First Published in 2022

TABLE OF CONTENT

INTRODUCTION **11**

CHAPTER 1: WHAT IS GASTRIC BAND HYPNOSIS **15**
- What is the Gastric Band? 15
- What is Self-Hypnosis? 17
- How Does Self-Hypnosis Work? 20

CHAPTER 2: PROPER NUTRITION FOR A BETTER LIFE **23**
- What is Proper Nutrition? 23
- How Balance Affects Success 24
- How to Account for Special Circumstances 25

CHAPTER 3: A HEALTHY MINDSET **26**
- Why Your Mindset Matters 26
- Why You're Worth It 27
- What Loving Yourself Really Means 28
- Weight Loss is Not a Punishment 32
- Affirmations 35
- Mindful Eating 37
- Scheduling Your Meals 40
- Holding Yourself Accountable 42

CHAPTER 4: THE 4 GOLDEN RULES OF EATING **46**
- When You Are Hungry, Eat 46
- Eat What You Want, Not What You Think You Should Have . 46
- Eat Consciously and Enjoy Every Mouthful 47
- When You Think You Are Full, Stop Eating 47

CHAPTER 5: PRACTICAL WEIGHT LOSS ADVICE **49**
- Intermittent Fasting: 49
- Weight Loss: 51

Keto, Plant-Based, and Other Diets: *56*

CHAPTER 6: MAKING WAY FOR PROGRESS **58**

Prepare Your Kitchen *58*

Prepare Your Mind *59*

Prepare Your Journal *60*

Prepare Your Loved Ones *62*

Manage Expectations *63*

CHAPTER 7: MORE ON SELF-HYPNOSIS **65**

Relax Completely - The Progressive Technique *65*

Relax Completely - The Confusional Technique *66*

Finding Your Method *66*

Finding Mantras or Statements *71*

CHAPTER 8: HYPNOSIS MANTRAS AND METHODS **74**

Affirmations *74*

A Pragmatic Approach *75*

A Spiritual Approach *76*

An Emotional Approach *78*

A Warrior Approach *79*

CHAPTER 9: SELF-HYPNOSIS SCRIPTS **82**

Self-Hypnosis for Food Addiction and Positive Change *83*

Self-Hypnosis for Boosting Confidence ...... **Errore. Il segnalibro non è definito.**

Self-Hypnosis for Emotional Eating *91*

CHAPTER 10: MORE WEIGHT LOSS MANAGEMENT TECHNIQUES **99**

CHAPTER 11: FACTS & MYTHS ABOUT SELF-HYPNOSIS **134**

Myths *134*

Facts *137*

CHAPTER 12: FACTS & MYTHS ABOUT WEIGHT LOSS 139
   Myths 139
   Facts 151

CHAPTER 13: FREQUENTLY ASKED QUESTIONS 157
   About Weight Loss 157
   About Nutrition 163
   About Health 167
   About Self-Hypnosis 170

CHAPTER 14: LIVING YOUR BEST LIFE 174
   Basic Nutrition 174
   Healthy Habits 175
   Your Physical Health 177
   Physical Activity 178
   The Immune System and Nutrition 181
   Hydration's Role 183
   The Quality of Your Nutrition 185
   Achieving Balance 187
   Living Your Best Life 189

Recipes for Healthy Living 191

Breakfast Recipes 192
   Strawberries and Cream Oatmeal: 192
   Blueberry Peach Oatmeal: 193
   Fall Spiced Apple Cranberry Oatmeal: 195
   Cherry Almond Oatmeal: 196
   Apple Pie and Dates Oatmeal: 197
   Peanut Butter Cup Overnight Oats: 199
   Pumpkin Spice Latte Overnight Oats: 201

Homemade Pumpkin Spice: 202

Healthy Breakfast Smoothies: **203**

    Gut-Healing Aloe Smoothie: 207

    Aloe Strawberry Smoothie: 208

    Gorgeous Green Smoothie: 209

    Immune Booster Turmeric and Pineapple Smoothie: 210

    Glowing Skin Smoothie: 211

    Tropical Mango Booster Smoothie: 212

    Cacao Blueberry Smoothie: 213

    Apple and Spinach Kiwi Smoothie: 214

    Basic Breakfast Smoothie: 215

    Other Breakfast Favorites: 216

    Poached Egg and Smashed Avocado on Toast 216

    Low-Fat Feta Cheese Omelette 218

    Healthy Overnight Oatmeal 219

Lunch Recipes **221**

    Summer Allotment Salad with English Mustard Dressing: .. 221

    Charred Corn, Chicken & Tortilla Salad with Chipotle Yogurt Dressing: 222

    Roasted Beetroot & Raw Honey Salad: 224

    Quinoa, Goat's Cheese & Peach Salad: 225

    Green Goddess Chicken Salad: 226

    Herby Orzo & Lemon Salad: 227

    Tomato & Mozzarella Salad with Tomato Dressing: 228

    Peach & Raspberry Fruit Salad with Mascarpone: 229

    Cauliflower Steaks with Roasted Red Pepper & Olive Salsa: 230

    Best Ever Potato Salad: 231

Roasted Asparagus and Pea Salad: 232
Healthy Waldorf Chicken Salad 233
Shaved Carrot and Radish Salad 234
Homemade Falafel 235
Moroccan-Style Chicken 237

Dinner Recipes **238**

Easy Chicken Soup 238
Healthy Broccoli Cheese Soup: 240
Carrot and Coriander Soup: 242
Thai Chicken Noodle Soup: 243
Tuscan Tomato Soup and Rosemary Garlic Croutons: 245
Pesto Minestrone Soup: 247
Leek and Butter Bean Soup with Kale and Bacon: 248
Lentil and Butternut Squash Spiced Soup: 249
Creamy Cauliflower Soup: 250
Celeriac Root Soup: 251
Broccoli and Pea Soup: 252
Supergreens Soup: 253
Chicken Broth Ramen with Salmon 254
Fish Tacos 256

Refined Sugar Free Treats: **258**

Chocolate Almond Cups: 258
Sugar-Free Protein Clinkers: 259
Sugar-free Chocolate and Sticky Date Pudding: 260
Warm Vanilla Coconut Sauce: 261
Rawmisu: 262
Honey and Lemon Curd Tart with Blueberries: 263

Honey and Lemon Curd:.. 263
Conclusion **264**

If you want to get the Free Audio version of the book, scan this QR Code

Introduction

Dear Reader,

You've recently made a pretty big decision regarding your lifestyle and your health, haven't you? Or, if you haven't quite made the decision yet, you're thinking very seriously about it. First and foremost, let me congratulate you for making that step; it is often one of the hardest.

Making the decision to change eveything about your lifestyle to yield a better result for your health and your quality of life is one that a lot of people dance around and avoid. This isn't for lack of discipline or because they don't want their lives to be better, mind you. It's simply a very large subject to broach and it bears a lot of emotional weight with it.

Weight loss has become such a tricky and entangled subject for millions of people across the globe. Many of our relationships with food have been based on some kind of disordered thought process that has led us into questionable territory health-wise.

Crash diets and conflicting information from all corners of social media have left a good number of us absolutely drowning in a sea of confusion. Those of us who wish to put in the work, make the changes, and start making better decisions for our bodies are left to wonder how we're really supposed to start. Surely cutting back and hitting the gym cannot be the only answers. Surely those of us who still feel hungry after a salad still have some hope?

We absolutely do. It turns out that the key to our weight loss might be a little bit closer to home than we initially anticipated. As one might be able to figure, one's relationship with food develops at a very young stage when parents and other adults in our lives influence many of our thoughts and perceptions. As a result of this, we can be saddled with a whole trove of conclusions, confusions, prejudices, and other things that can shape your connection to food.

Hypnosis is an incredibly powerful tool that one can use to access those things that are hidden from our conscious selves. Once they're revealed, you can use suggestions, mantras, and causative thought processes to help you to unravel or replace the things that have been holding you back from making the strides toward your weight loss goals that you've been working for.

It is a common misconception by people with no excess weight to lose that those who are overweight simply aren't trying hard enough to lose those pounds. That simply isn't the case and all the work that you've done up to this point is completely valid. It's all been a part of the journey that led you here, to the greatest tool for the job.

In this book, you will find some of the most thoughtfuly-prepared tips and solutions to help you in your efforts toward a healthier, more confident lifestyle. You'll find brass-tacks information that will show you how to approach proper nutrition and your weight loss goals so they make sense for you and your life, and so you're satisfied with your meals and your progress.

You'll find key information compiled to give you the best possible approach to weight loss without any of the assumptions that are made by diet books. Diet books make a lot of assumptions about works for everyone, when there is no blanket solution that works for every individual.

You're a whole person with wants, needs, thoughts, feelings, and you differ greatly from even the person closest to you. What works for you may simply not work for someone else, and vice versa.

That is why this book contains information and approaches that you can tailor to the lifestyle and the goals *you* want. Whether you're someone who likes a more emotional approach to such issues or whether you're a through-and-through pragmatist, there is information in this book that will see you through even the most troublesome parts of the weight loss journey.

It's this book that can bring you a more thorough understanding of the things that are truly holding you back in life. You may sit and think about the things that hold you back, and you may even come up with a hundred and one answers as to why, but until you address those insidious things that linger beneath the surface, it's going to feel utterly impossible for you to really get the fast and lasting kind of progress you've really been searching for until now.

Taking care of the mental aspects of weight loss might seem like one of those things that can wait or potentially go unaddressed for life, but it's so important to realize that just because it's not visible, doesn't mean it's not profoundly affecting your life and your ability to be happy.

While you have this book in your possession, you are holding the key to your own future. You have the power to make the changes you've been dreaming about every time you look in the mirror. You have the power to say what dress size you'll be by this time next year, and you have the power to make yourself happier along the way than you've been in a very long time. Why would you want to put off something like that?

While I have you here, engaged with me, I want to impress upon you the importance of action and self-love. What you are considering doing right now is a consideration born of self-love and self-interest. Something there is not enough of in the common person these days. You deserve to be happy, to be healthy, to be confident, and to be free of the things that have held you back for so long.

Keep reading today and make your plans for health, for weight loss, and for positive change for the better in your life. Turn the page, and in so doing, turn over a new leaf in your life.

Here is to you, dear reader, in your pursuit of everlasting health and true happiness!

Chapter 1: What is Gastric Band Hypnosis

What is the Gastric Band?

Many people, when they are considering their options for weight loss, are presented with the possibility of weight loss surgery. This is especially the case if the person has a considerable amount of weight to lose. More than 50 extra pounds on a person can be a tall order for traditional diet and exercise, though it is absolutely possible to do so. If they have difficulty getting their progress really moving, modern surgical methods exist to motivate and steer you in the right direction, should you need such assistance.

The gastric band or laparoscopic band is a type of bariatric (the branch of medicine that deals with obesity and its causes) surgery that allows the patient to feel as though they have undergone gastric bypass surgery without some of the incisions and recovery time required of such a procedure. The band is an adjustable object that is placed around the entirety of the stomach to constrict the clearance that food has to pass through your body. In such a procedure, the band would be used to drastically reduce the size of the stomach so patients for this surgery feel much fuller on far smaller portions of food. Appetite management and suppression can be huge keys for weight loss success.

This minimally-invasive procedure is preferred by some because it is a surgery that can be done very quickly and that is reversible and adjustable to suit the needs of each individual patient. It serves as a helpful guide and tool to allow patients to get their appetite under control without the commitment of a permanent adjustment to their stomach structure, as would be the case with something like a sleeve gastrectomy or a gastric bypass. Other methods for appetite suppression can be cause for concern from some doctors, as they are often stimulants that can cause some other complications, and which can throw off the patient's blood pressure.

In patients of a particularly large size, high blood pressure is a concern that can arise naturally. Having excess weight, excess salt and fat intake, and having low activity levels are all risk factors for heart issues and high blood pressure. Because of this, appetite suppressing medications can be a risky route for larger patients to take, putting their health in a questionable position until their weight can be reduced. This is why the surgery can be a helpful tool. There are some other types of weight loss surgery that are a little bit more intensive or effective for certain patients. We'll go into what those are here. The next step up in intensity on the scale of bariatric surgery options would be the *sleeve gastrectomy*. This procedure requires an incision up the side of the stomach and a removal of a large portion of the stomach, leaving a tube-like length behind so the stomach can contain about 20-30% as much as it did prior to the procedure. This is very effective surgery for larger patients, and it has been known to produce excellent weight loss results for those who need some help curbing their appetite.

There are some dietary restrictions that are put into place for the patient after this procedure. In the very beginning of recovery, intake should be kept light, but gradually, after recovering for several weeks, the gradual introduction of solid and mild foods will begin.

The next, more intense step in bariatric surgery would be the gastric bypass. This is a procedure that removes up to 90% of the stomach, leaving only a very small portion of the organ in the body so that portion intake is drastically reduced for the patient. From the time of surgery, intake is drastically altered and reduced to allow the body to acclimate to the new manner of operating.

Liquid diets following bariatric surgery are quite common as they allow the stomach to feel full without putting too much strain on the sutures newly put in place on the stomach. As the incisions begin to heal, more foods can be introduced over time, graduating from soft foods to something more solid. This could take several weeks and following your doctor's instructions is always the first step to the most ideal recovery for you.

From then on, patients who have had either the sleeve gastrectomy or the gastric bypass will need to make special accommodations in the way that they eat, making sure not to drink or eat too much at any one time. In addition to this, the patient will need to make sure that they're not taking on too many small meals throughout the day, as the calories from those small meals can add up and hinder weight loss progress during the healing process and beyond.

The gastric band is often looked at as an optimal option for someone who isn't certain that the full bariatric surgery would be for them. The patient is still given every bit of weight loss help that they would otherwise be getting, without having to worry about as many incisions and as lengthy a healing process. Bariatric surgery is often considered to be a method of weight loss intervention to help patients to make immediate and drastic changes to their lifestyles that allow them to lose a significant amount of weight in a fairly short period of time. From then on, it becomes the duty of the patient to adopt some healthy habits that will allow them to continue their weight loss and to keep the weight off for the rest of their lives following surgery. Those tips and methods will be covered in this book, so keep reading for your ultimate guide to effective, sustained, and permanent weight loss!

What is Self-Hypnosis?

Most of the time, when we think of hypnosis, we think of some parlor trick wherein an entertaining man in a cape dangles a watch, puts someone into a trance, and makes them do something silly like clucking like a chicken. Now, of course, this is not the kind of thing we're talking about when we suggest using hypnosis as a form of therapy. Hypnosis is a therapy process and technique that has proven to have some fairly surprising positive results.

You will often find that the usefulness and the appropriate place for hypnosis to be a subject of some dispute. In this section, we'll describe what hypnosis is and what it aims to achieve. Then we'll discuss what we mean by "self-hypnosis," and how the two subjects differentiate.

In the beginning of a hypnotherapy regimen, your therapist will typically go over your goals for the process, discuss expectations from either side, and answer any questions that you might have about the process. From there, your therapist will seek to make you as comfortable as possible so they can relax you completely. This can be done with verbal cues, motions, and a number of other means. You and your doctor can discuss an option that would work best for you.

The goal of these repetitions is to put you into a state that is somewhat like a trance. In that trance your body will become completely relaxed and your mind will become receptive to commands and suggestions that your therapist has chosen based on your goals for the therapy.

Once you've completed the session, your therapist will bring you back into the present moment and full consciousness before addressing what was covered and sending you on your way.

For a select few people, one session of hypnosis will set them on the right track and help them achieve their goals. For many others, therapists recommend starting with five sessions, then determining from there what you need in order to achieve your therapy goals.

Some have been discouraged to learn that hypnotism simply doesn't work for them. They're unable to follow those cues and achieve complete relaxation as a result of them. The unfortunate truth is that many people experience this, so be sure to be open, honest, and communicative with your therapist about the things that do and do not work to help you. There are those who claim that the positive results from hypnotherapy are little more than a placebo effect, but it's hard to argue when the patients have seen such a marked improvement in their lives and when their therapy goals have become reachable through this practice. In mental health, it's important to reach for the things that make sense *for you* and which are effective *for you*. It's one of those things where you have to push yourself to be self-minded. It doesn't matter if Tom from work thinks it's a load of bunk, it doesn't matter if Shelly in your bowling team is telling everyone that she heard that her sister's friend's cousin's coworker now squawks uncontrollably at the sound of a bell, and it doesn't matter if your own family isn't sure that it will work. What matters is if *you* get good results from it and that *you* feel better when you practice it.

Now, let's talk about *self*-hypnosis, which is a teeny bit different than hypnosis. The major difference is that you don't have a therapist there working with you to read your face, to listen to your words, and to give you prompts to delve into your subconscious. These things can be very helpful for some, while they are nothing more than a distraction to others. This means it's very important to keep an open and honest line of communication with your therapist so you can tell them exactly what you're experiencing so they can help you determine the best course of action to proceed.

When you're doing self-hypnosis, you're taking care of all of these aspects by yourself. You're staying aware of what you're doing while still completely relaxing yourself. This sounds harder than it really is, don't run away screaming just yet!

The practice of self-hypnosis means that you're going to become highly focused on and absorbed in the experience of it while you're doing it. In addition to this, you're going to be giving yourself positive suggestions about your goals, ways to reach them, your outlook, or even just about self-view. These positive suggestions depend solely on what your goals are for your hypnosis regimen. If you're looking to focus on your work ethic, you'll want your suggestions to be centered on that topic. If you're hoping to be a more positive person, your affirmations should reflect that as well.

This practice can be highly empowering, as it puts the control of your thoughts and your whole thought process in the palm of your hand. With this tool, you can change your line of thinking to match what you think would be the most beneficial to your goals.

For instance, if you feel like you could do so much better at connecting with people if you could just get out of your own head once in a while and if you could stop thinking so negatively about yourself while you're connecting with them, you could use your suggestions during self-hypnosis to make your self-talk more positive. Instead of thinking things like, *They're never going to find you interesting,* you can think things like, *Everyone is unique and you're no different!* Or *I have something to offer these people and I'm going to figure out what it is.* Pick the suggestions that would apply most to you and that would resonate with you. It's all about *you!*

How Does Self-Hypnosis Work?

The work of Sigmund Freud put forth the idea that the human mind is more or less split into three distinct, yet connected parts. The first part of the mind is known as the **Conscious Mind**. The conscious mind is the top, most accessible, and more frequented portion of the mind. It's the area of the mind that is responsible for conscious thinking and for making sense of the things of which we are directly and immediately aware.

For instance, you are in traffic and someone cuts you off. You see this, you put your foot on the brake, and you say a few choice words about it. You are directly aware of that incident happening in front of you and you processed it on the conscious level.

The next layer of the mind is the **Subconscious Mind** This is the part of the mind that is just below the conscious level. It's listening and taking note without really analyzing anything that it's taking in. It can affect the way we react to certain things and it can even affect how we think about them.

So let's go back to the incident in traffic. On a conscious level, you have seen that person cut you off. You have applied the brake and you've continued to drive. Now, on a subconscious level, your mind is thinking about the other incidents that seem similar to this one. It wants to react to them in a similar way that you have before. This can result in you screaming in your car about it until you feel better, laying on the horn and taking out your anger that way, or it could leave you feeling terrified of traffic in general, or it could have any one of about a million other effects on you, depending on what your past experiences have been.

The subconscious mind is responsible for a lot of things that we say and do without really thinking about them. It's always listening for the things that we hear from others, for the things that we tell ourselves, and for the experiences that we go through on a daily basis.

The subconscious mind is the one we're talking to when we give ourselves affirmations each day. We're telling that part of our mind some positive things that we would like to make true throughout our lives, and we're getting the help of our subconscious minds to help us behave in the correct manner to bring about those things. We'll cover more about this in Chapter 3.

The final layer of the mind is the **Unconscious Mind**. This is the part of your mind that holds stuff that very rarely ever comes to the surface. Repressed things, traumas, and suppressed memories end up here as sort of a holding place for the mind. It can be accessed with the help of a therapist and those memories and incidents should be dealt with using the help of a certified professional.

The reason hypnotism works is because with that total relaxation that you achieve in the very beginning, you're given access to the deeper parts of the mind and you're put in control of rewriting some of the things that are in there. The conclusions we never even knew we reached about our own capabilities, the negative thoughts that have held us back from ending up where we wanted, and the imposed conclusions from friends and family that have made us feel like less than we truly are can all be accessed and rectified with the use of hypnosis. These are all things you will find on the subconscious level of the mind, which can also be accessed through self-hypnosis.

Once you're able to fully relax yourself, you can make the right suggestions for you and your goals. Those suggestions will impinge on your subconscious mind and allow you to shift any conclusions or computations from that portion of mind that have previously held you back.

Chapter 2: Proper Nutrition for a Better Life

What is Proper Nutrition?

Proper nutrition is something that is often talked about when weight loss comes into the equation. In many cases, proper nutrition isn't quite specified or defined, so I'm going to take the time to clear that up right now! Proper nutrition, quite simply, means that your diet is giving you plenty of nutrients, vitamins, and minerals that it needs to function at its best. This is achieved by having a diverse meal plan filled with plenty of protein, veggies, fruits, whole grains, and supplements. Keeping track of your calories and your nutrients is a great way to make sure you're getting enough of everything.

When you're dieting, you must make sure that you're getting the right nutrients for your body and your lifestyle. If you're starving yourself or exclusively eating foods that aren't beneficial for you, then you're not going to have an easy time of being successful in your endeavors. You're going to feel sluggish, faint, or worse and sustaining it will be virtually impossible.

There are so many diets out there that encourage people to eat too little in a short time period to "jumpstart" the weight loss process. There are diets that encourage people to eat as few as 500 calories per day for up to three weeks at a time. Doing this will literally starve your body and leave your body scrambling to pull together nutrients from just about anywhere. Yes, this means utilizing fat stores in your body, but it does it on a starvation basis, which doesn't teach your body how to handle a healthy lifestyle. The moment you go back to eating 1,800-2,000 calories per day, your body is going to pack on those pounds.

Proper nutrition is needed for *lifestyle change*, which is the best possible way to shed excess weight and to keep it from coming back ever again. Simply plan meals that fall in line with your goals, take care of your mental state, and adopt those into your daily and weekly routines. That is the best way to live a healthy life and to get what you want from your weight loss regimen.

How Balance Affects Success

Balance is the key to success. Remember that, repeat it to yourself, write it on sticky notes and plaster them all over your house. Balance is the best possible way to make sure that you're getting everything you need from your diet and indeed from life itself. If you're focusing too hard on one thing, that means you're not focusing enough on the others. Some things outweigh others, so you need less of them, this is what we mean by *balance*. Take into account the things that are more nutritionally weighted and cut back on those!

You want small amounts of things like animal fats and dairy, but you want large amounts of big, leafy greens! Nutritionally, the animal fats take up a lot more calories and they can take up more of your daily calorie budget. You want to fill in with those veggies, because they take up less of your calories, but they provide more nutritional benefit per serving.

It will take some time for you to find balance in your diet. You will need to figure out which of the foods you want to cut down, which foods you want to increase, and which foods you wish to cut out completely. Being a picky eater can save you a lot of time, trouble, and calories if you're looking for places to cut down!

If you have plenty of delicious and nutritious foods in your diet, you can introduce a little bit of the more indulgent foods here and there without too much trouble. This means that you're not all feast or famine with your dieting options. You get to have a bit of everything that you like, but you're doing so in balance, so you're not negatively impacting your weight loss goals when you do it!

How to Account for Special Circumstances

Life is full of occasions to eat. Birthdays, anniversaries, celebrations, and more will lead us to the dinner table with our families, looking for those comforting foods with lots of things in them that we shouldn't eat all the time. There is nothing wrong, however, with the occasional indulgence. You should know that you don't have to deny yourself the chance to go out and be with your family because you're trying to be healthy and eat well for yourself. There are some things you can do that will allow you to have that outing with your family without feeling held back by your ambitions to do better for yourself health-wise.

If you know in advance that you're going to be spending an evening out with family and friends, the best thing you can do is lighten your load throughout the day leading up to it so that when you do indulge a little bit, you're not sent completely overboard.

This doesn't mean that you have to starve yourself, but it does mean that you should stick to your serving sizes for breakfast and lunch and that your snacks should be small, modest, and healthy when you do have them. Bring some carrot sticks, some nuts, or some other healthy snack that you like so you don't feel like you're depriving yourself, but so you also feel like you're keeping up on top of your daily calories.

There are some more helpful tips about eating out at restaurants in Chapter 10 of this book!

Chapter 3: A Healthy Mindset

Why Your Mindset Matters

Dieting and feeling like you're constantly on a roller coaster of self-esteem and food difficulties can make you feel really negative if you're not careful. Many of us have a casual hatred toward the foods we actually love because we have been made to think that "they make us fat." Many of us have internalized negative feelings because we think that excess weight on our bodies somehow makes us less worthy as people.

Your mindset has so much of an impact on your weight loss. If you're feeling negative, you're feeling brooding, or you're even feeling like you're dieting as some sort of punishment, it's never going to pay off. People generally thrive under positive circumstances and putting someone (yourself included) into a regimen of negative feedback and activity is going to eventually make the person quit, or it's going to make the issue even worse.

It's so important for you to realize that you *are* worth the effort, for you to realize that dieting and weight loss are not punishments, and that loving yourself is really the biggest factor to your being able to lose the weight you want to lose. Hating your body and talking badly about yourself only creates a self-fulfilling prophecy of failure, negativity, and weight gain. It's imperative that you frequently remind yourself that you are a good person, that you are a worthy person, and that you are not the sum of your mistakes. This should come before *anything*, including the conclusion that you need to lose weight. These things are always true and you must know them before you undertake any new changes in your life and even before conducting yourself in daily life.

These are inherent truths about you and knowing them and asserting them will take you where you want to go in life. Having a negative mindset will lead you right to the bottom of a pit that you can never seem to get out of and you're going to be struggling with your self-image and your self-esteem more than anything else. You can't focus on making delicious foods, making a lifestyle that you love, and loving yourself if you have already decided that you're not worth any of the trouble that goes into those things.

So before you undertake anything else—before you start any other regimens, work on your mindset. Affirm for yourself that you deserve the best and that you deserve all the positive results that will come about from weight loss, increased personal health, and from loving yourself. You are worth the time, you are worth the effort, and you are going to knock your own socks off when you realize all the things of which you're capable!

Why You're Worth It

People can tell you all day long that you are worth it, that you are unique, that you mean something to them, that you are a valuable person who deserves everything you've been striving to achieve, and you still won't believe it. Not fully. Knowing that you're worth it is something that has to come from within you. I'm going to tell you in this section that you are indeed worth it and why, and it's up to you to make yourself believe it over time. I want you to make that a huge priority. Getting help with the things that you want to change in your life is only really possible and sustainable if you believe in it, and if you don't have any subconscious notions that you shouldn't achieve or that you don't deserve to achieve the intended end results.

Each person is unique in their own way. Every single one of us is born with a completely unique set of traits, mannerisms, notions, dreams, inclinations, idiosyncrasies, and so much more. Each of these things coalesce to make someone who adds to the tapestry of life in this world we live in. Each one of us deserves to be content, healthy, and to follow the things that bring us health and happiness.

You have spent a decent number of years on this Earth, making sure that you're following the basic rules of society and the groups that you're in, right? You've done your best not to hurt others, you've made a couple mistakes here and there, but by and large, you've done your best to be a good person. That's all it takes to be worthy of health and happiness. That is the only thing.

So if you have lived some years on this earth, if you have been kind to others, if you have struggled through some things, and if you desire to lose the weight, then you are *worth it*. Now all that's left for you to do is reach out and take that weight loss for yourself.

It can be hard, if you're used to serving others or putting others' needs before your own, to put yourself in the center of your focus and do the things you know must be done in order to benefit you.

You have to convince yourself that you are as worthy and as important to you as all the people around you are. If you know you would drop everything to help a friend who was struggling with their self image and their weight, you should be willing to do the same for yourself. Ask yourself for help and be your own greatest asset in pulling off the unthinkable.

Take the time to think of yourself from an outsider's perspective. "[Your name] sure is helpful. I've seen them help people before and it seems like they're a really good person. They're having some trouble right now and I think I could give it to them. Let me see what I can do to help in their situation." Resolve to allocate your emotional energies and resources for yourself and *use them*. You are capable of helping so many people and there is no earthly reason why you shouldn't be among that group.

What Loving Yourself Really Means

Loving yourself means something different to each and every person. This is part of why it's so hard for me to tell you *how* to love yourself, but I promise you that I'm going to do my best. You can find a lot of different statements about loving yourself in many different places. Some people will tell you that it doesn't matter how much you weigh, it doesn't matter what you look like, and that loving yourself means always being kind to yourself in spite of everything.

I'm here to overturn those notions a little bit, but I'm going to start by saying *those are not incorrect*. There is just a little bit more to consider here. Loving yourself means exactly the same thing as loving someone else and pretending like it's different because it's you is where the pitfalls lie. Let's talk about someone you know. His name is Tony, he is 33 years old, he lives with his mother, and his motivation is a little bit lacking. His mother is starting to lose money from her retirement because she has to pay for the mortgage and her hours at work have been scaled back. Tony was supposed to get a job that would have helped to pay for the difference, but he missed his interview and he hasn't seemed motivated to go for another. He seems depressed because his life has no direction and his indecision about a next move has paralyzed him.

Now, Tony is a great friend of yours. You have known him since you were both teenagers, he's helped you move, he's been there in the middle of the night for you when things have gone sour and no one else was awake. He stood up at your best friend's wedding and gave a heartfelt speech with plenty of tastefully-timed jokes. He is a decent person who is clearly struggling and you have much love for him in your heart.

How do you handle this situation with him? Do you hover over his shoulder and constantly tell him that he should be doing more, that he's not worth the help anyone could give him, and then tell him that his mother secretly (but not so secretly) resents him for his burden? This is the same thing as you telling yourself "I haven't made moves on my goals. I am worthless." See how when it's done to someone other than yourself, it just seems cruel? Some might call it "tough love," but it's not. That type of behavior is just cruel.

Now, if you do want to go the tough love route with Tony, the way to do it would be to go visit him. Talk with him and get down to brass tacks about what's going on around him, what he can and should be doing about it, then attempt to help him solve it.

A good way to approach this kind of scenario with a tough love attitude would be saying something like, "I wanted to give you the space to figure this out on your own, but now I'm getting concerned about you and I want to help. Your mom is starting to struggle and I know you would never want that. How can I help you make a choice on your next move and what can I do to support you making that next move? Either way, we have to get a move on soon because this situation has to change. You know I love you, but this can't keep going like this."

Doing this shows that you're not attacking him. You put a lot of verbal emphasis on your care for him and you come to him with the offering of your help rather than just telling him to figure it out.

Now, if you were to focus a productive tough love statement inward, it would sound something like, "I've been through a lot and I've been struggling. It's time to make the right move now and I have got to figure out what it is because I don't want to keep living like this. Do I need help with this or is it something I can do by myself?" Answer this last question honestly. If you need help, you owe it to yourself to get it. Struggling by without it when you need it is pointless and a waste of time.

The next approach to consider is a much softer, kinder one. Based on your relationship with Tony, you will know which approach will suit him better and leave him feeling more empowered to do something about the situation. This is the nurturing, loving approach that tells Tony that you love him and that you want to see him succeed because he deserves it. That might sound a little something like this: "Listen, Tony. I'm worried about you because I've been watching struggle lately and it hurts me to see you like this. I know that you have some ambitions and I want to help you work out what they are; let's talk a little bit about what you want from life and see if we can figure out what your next move should be. Is there anything immediate stopping you? Questions you need answered or resources you feel like you need but don't have?" Turning that kind of question inward does get you thinking about the things that have been holding you back and keeping you from reaching your potential. If you are simply trying to get going, but there is something missing or some unseen roadblock like this, asking yourself questions about what exactly it is could be helpful. Consider also talking it out with someone. Sometimes it's not until you're trying to explain your position to someone else that you really realize what that position is.

You can see from the examples above that loving Tony means going up to him, being direct, being kind, and getting to the nitty gritty so you can help him to get something positive happening in his life for him and for his mother.

You know, as a friend, that talking to him in a rude manner and tearing him down is never going to empower him enough to get him moving. You know that beating him over the head with his shortcomings is only going to make him feel worse and has the potential to just set him back in his efforts. The same is true for you. If you're so busy telling yourself that you're a bad person because of your shortcomings, that you're no good because of the troubles that you've had in your life, and that you've wasted too much time on whatever you've been going through, then you're just going to push yourself to a complete stop. You're going to motivate yourself to do nothing and continue feeling horrible about all of the above.

It doesn't matter how much truth there is in the negative self-talk that you use. It's time to do away with it, because *that* goes against loving yourself. Loving yourself means being there for you, caring what happens to you, and doing whatever it takes to help yourself be happy because that's what it means to love anyone.

You don't have to accept that you are overweight, you don't have to look in the mirror and hug yourself on the days when you don't feel quite like you love yourself, and you don't have to do anything outlandishly silly to achieve love of self. You simply have to care. You have to talk positively to yourself, and you have to demand change of yourself when you know it's for the better.

You would demand that Tony take better care of himself if he needed to do so. You would demand that any of your other friends take care of their own physical health if it was at risk, and you would love any member of your family in spite of their body type, outlook, self-image, or difficulty. That is all loving yourself means and you need to start practicing. Get good at recognizing when you're being mean to yourself and stand up for yourself.

"You are worthless."

"Hey! That's not okay. I am worth plenty and I deserve to be happy. Stop telling me untrue and unkind things like that."

You owe yourself that much.

Weight Loss is Not a Punishment

A mistake that many people make is thinking of diets as "a punishment for being fat," when that couldn't be further from the truth. The first issue in this is thinking about diets as a short-term thing. Diets should be a change in lifestyle that allow you to look and feel your best at all times. The second issue with this is thinking that being overweight warrants a punishment. It doesn't.

Being overweight is not a crime, it's not an affront to anyone, it's not an offense for which you need to apologize. It's not even something you should have to feel guilty about. It's something that happens to everyone at some point or another in their lives. We all have those vacations, occasions, or rough spots that lead to our eating a bit more than we should for a time, which leads to a little bit of excess on our bodies. Now, for some people this is not a big deal and it can be easily reversed. For some, it's the start of a steady gain, and for others, that excess just kind of sits there as they get back to normalcy, sitting in purgatory never to be lost or added to. Everyone is different.

Losing weight is something that you can and should do when you need to. It's not something that everyone should be striving for all the time. The ideal situation is for you to be at an ideal weight for you as established by you and your doctor. Once you reach that weight, you maintain it by eating a healthy number of calories that are balanced with the right nutrients each day. You aren't dieting at that point, you're simply living on a regimen like normal.

Now, if you are thinking that you can do a diet for a while, lose the weight, then get back to eating indulgent foods at every meal, knocking back 3,000+ calories each day without any repercussions, I'm afraid you're going to have to ditch that notion. The only situation in which maintaining this number of calories throughout the day is feasible is if you are an athlete, but even then the calories that you're consuming will need to be of a certain quality. Bodies by cheese puffs are rarely healthy and attempting this regimen should be avoided if at all possible.

It's incredibly important for you to see excess weight for what it is. Excess weight. It's fat. It's not a curse, it's not a crime, it's not a failure. It's just your body holding on to potential energy that is waiting to be burned. There is very little point to feeling guilty about gaining excess weight. It slows you down, it's no fun feeling that way, and you haven't done anything wrong.

There are a lot of conclusions about gained weight that are imposed by societal standards and media that can throw your eyes off the prize. Foods that are low-calorie or low-fat are marketed as "guilt-free," television characters talk about eating more than they ought to and hating themselves for it, body standards are all over the place, and the average people are left in the middle thinking that everyone around them isn't struggling with the exact same issues. We are left thinking that if we put on a couple of extra pounds, everyone around us is going to vilify us and make us feel like an outcast for it. There are many things you could do with your life that are far worse than putting on a couple of pounds.

Losing weight that you've gained isn't something you have to be upset about, it's not something that is meant to deprive you, hurt you, or cause you shame. Dieting and losing weight is about keeping your health goals in mind, and it's about helping you to find the right nutrient balance that works to keep you going through your day. The best diet is the one that you can continue for the rest of your life to help you with maintenance. The right number of calories with the right balance of nutrients, and just enough fun foods throughout to keep life interesting and to keep you from feeling deprived.

The indulgent foods are meant to be consumed in moderation, so you want to make sure that you're not banking on having lots and lots of those for any sustained period of time. Take the holidays for instance. There are lots of parties with plenty of rich, indulgent foods. Thanks to the holidays, we have access to lots of cookies, cakes, sides, starches, fats, creamy foods, etc., that remind us of that lovely time of year. It is also typical for people to start up a bunch of crash diets just a couple weeks later at the beginning of the new year!

Think about going into the holidays without too much excess weight on you. You indulge and have your holiday snacks and meals (as is tradition), and then when they're over, you go back to your normal pattern of eating. You lower your calories just a little bit, maybe amp up the activity a little bit, and before you know it, those extra pounds are gone with very little effort on your part. It's not a big to-do to get it done, and you don't feel like you've got those dieting trends bearing down on you, keeping you from just enjoying your days while the weight works its way out of your system.

If you can get your head on straight about your weight loss and health goals, see them as nothing more than items on a to-do list, take all the pressure, emotion, misconceptions, and outside opinions out of it, you're going to find it leaps and bounds easier to deal with it. I *know* this is so much easier said than done, so I don't want you to think that I don't see the intricacies and difficulties that are part and parcel to this task. This is something you can affirm with yourself, though.

"It doesn't matter how long it takes, so long as it gets done."
"I am more than the number on the scale."
"Society doesn't get to tell me how and when to be healthy."
Some of these statements might work for you to hear them every day. It can absolutely help to put things into the right perspective for yourself and to give your conscious mind some more, healthier perspectives on the subject of weight loss.

Affirmations

Affirmations are an incredibly effective self-help tool. They might sound silly to you and in fact, you may have seen shows or movies making fun of people who use them. The fact of the matter is that doing the same affirmations daily for a period of time will allow you to impinge on your subconscious mind. That is what makes them effective.

We talked a little bit in Chapter 1 about the subconscious mind and how it works. The subconscious mind is not a part of your mind that learns. It's a part of the mind that listens and records. It makes note of the things that it hears the most often or in moments when it's feeling particularly receptive and it holds onto those so that when it sees a thought process in your conscious mind where it can fit something in, it does so.

Let's take an example that hits close to home. Let's say that you constantly make jokes about being depressed. You tell people often "I am depressed," or when someone compliments you, your response is "Thanks, it's the depression." It's funny at first, but your subconscious mind takes that to heart. It hears, "I am depressed," so often that it enforces it. It makes certain that it is true.

Now, before anyone misunderstands and thinks that I'm saying depression is self-made, let me be clear. You can absolutely be depressed because of other factors and that is between you and your doctor. However, you can enforce that depression on yourself without even realizing it.

Instead of saying, "I am depressed," or "I have depression," you can simply amend a little bit. Say things like, "I'm dealing with my depression in healthy ways," or "I am not letting depression take control." If someone asks or if it becomes relevant, rather than just offering that you have it, you can say, "I am working through depression."

Now, when it comes to weight loss, your subconscious mind may have quite a few conflicting notions that are keeping you from being in control. Weight loss doesn't have to be hard, but it often is hard because of these things. Knowing what they are will take some doing, but you should at least be able to put some other positive statements in there until you and a therapist can work through what's already there.

Come up with 2 or 3 really great affirmations about your goals for your weight loss. I'm going to list some affirmations here, but you don't have to pick any from this list. Just come up with or find a phrase that strikes a chord with you and that you want in your heart of hearts to believe over time.

1. I don't eat when I don't need to.
2. I am being healthy and getting great results.
3. I don't need food to cope.
4. My weight is healthy and getting healthier every day.
5. Losing weight is something that comes naturally to me.
6. Achieving my weight loss goals brings me joy.
7. By giving my body what it needs, it will give me health.
8. I am losing weight every day and feeling great doing it.
9. I am worthy of achieving my goals and I'm doing it day by day.
10. By eating things that are good for my body, I am showing myself I care.
11. Today I will conquer my health goals with ease.
12. I have the strength to resist temptation and to spoil myself with healthy food.
13. Positive energy in me is bringing my goals to life.
14. The things I want are within reach.
15. My goal weight is getting closer every single day.
16. I love moving my body to achieve my fitness goals.

17. My mind and body are healthy and getting stronger every day.
18. I can keep myself fit with little effort.
19. Fitness, clean eating, and a healthy lifestyle come easily to me.
20. I deserve to look and feel the way I want.
21. I love my body and I take care of it every day.
22. Being a healthy weight comes naturally to me.
23. I easily choose healthy foods over indulgent ones.
24. Living a healthy lifestyle brings me joy.
25. I find it easy to be disciplined with my meals.
26. I love to snack on fruits and veggies instead of processed stuff.
27. I find exercise freeing and fulfilling.
28. I am always creating new, healthy habits
29. Weight loss comes to me effortlessly.
30. I am only hungry three times a day.
31. I only eat when I am hungry.
32. I don't suffer from food cravings
33. I am in control of my appetite and cravings.
34. Junk food doesn't bring me joy.
35. Healthy food brings me joy.
36. I love my exercise regimen.
37. I enjoy pushing my body's fitness boundaries and expanding them each day.
38. I lose weight without trying.
39. My body is thriving.
40. My goal weight is within reach.

Mindful Eating

Mindful eating is a great way to keep tabs on everything you're eating. Let me paint a picture of a scenario for you in which mindful eating could come in handy. Let's say that you've had a long day at work and your boss was really getting after you about some of the nitty gritty details of your work. She seemed to be hanging on every single detail of your work and nitpicked right up until it was time for you to leave, then she asked for you to stay behind a few minutes late so you could wrap up the final details of a project before you went. This means that your schedule for the evening was thrown off a little bit.

Exhausted from the day and a little frazzled from being micromanaged, you head home to make yourself some dinner, unwind from the day, and take some time for yourself. You get home and you peek in the fridge to find that you have many healthy ingredients that you have to slice up, prepare, and cook for yourself. Nothing can just be thrown in the microwave so you can head to the couch and plant yourself there for the evening.

You go into the cabinet and you grab a snack, maybe some chips to take the edge off until you can get up the energy to cook. You figure, *why bother with a bowl? It'll just be another dish to wash*, and you head to the couch with the bag. You turn on the television and before you know it, you've got the empty chip bag on the sofa next to you and your stomach is growling at you for something more substantial. The thought of getting up and cooking something isn't all that appealing, so you just decide to order in. *It'll be my cheat meal for the week*, but you forgot that you ordered in two nights ago after a meeting ran long.

Sitting in front of the television with your dinner, you munch down and just a few minutes later, you're all done. Your meal is gone without a trace (except the bag it came in) and you still feel a little bit… Unsatisfied. Or maybe you've got the opposite problem and you feel bloated from all that food all at once.

Either way, you're the victim of mindless eating and a negative outcome as a result. You've eaten entirely too many calories and the fresh veggies in your refrigerator are left for another day, increasing the chances that they will go uneaten before they turn or wilt.

Let's take a look at how this day would go if you were eating mindfully as a matter of principle. Your boss has put you through the ringer and now you've arrived home late. You open the refrigerator and you see that you've prepped some meals ahead because you learned from that meeting that ran late two nights ago. Being mindful of what you eat, being completely present and thinking clearly when you made your menu decisions, gave you the right perspective and the strength to compensate.

You pop your leftover spanish rice with smothered chicken into the microwave along with that side of steamed squash and while it's cooking, you pour yourself a little glass of wine. In just a couple of minutes, you've got yourself set up for a lovely dinner and you're able to take joy in the things that you're watching on television. You're still being mindful, however, so you take a full 20 minutes to eat your meal. You make sure to chew your food for proper digestion and you savor each bite.

Once your dinner is over, you wash your couple of dishes and spend the rest of your evening doing other things that bring you joy. If you're hungry later on in the evening, you pour yourself a small serving of those chips and continue going about your evening, not allowing a mindless consumption of those snacks become the centerpiece of your evening.

Now, mindful eating isn't going to overhaul your whole life or anything, but it is going to completely revolutionize your relationship with food. Food is something that many of us have taken to using like a habit or a vice. Eating food is not something that should be used to numb pain, to comfort, to fill time, to cure boredom, as a hobby, or as a sport. It's something that we do consciously to keep our bodies going.

If you have found that you often check out before you eat, take some time to reset your whole process. Don't eat in front of the television for a while. Don't bring your phone, a book, or any video games into your mealtimes and sit at the table. Sitting at your desk in front of your computer or sitting in front of the television will fix your attention on something other than the food.

For a little while, maybe a week or so, eat in that quiet space with maybe some background music to liven things up a little bit. Concentrate on eating your meal slowly and methodically. Don't take bites that are too big for you to swallow all at once, chew enough to allow your body to digest your food properly and optimally, and concentrate on taking about 20 minutes to get through the meal.

Too often, we swipe something on the go, scarf it down, and get onto the next thing. Alternatively, we settle in on the couch with a bunch of snacks and just chow down without realizing it until our hand swipes the bottom of the empty bag. No judgements; we've all been there. This is not a sustainable habit though, and it's not something you should try to do regularly. There is nothing wrong with doing it every once in a while, but it's a very unhealthy habit to keep that can stack up so many more calories that you might even realize when you're doing it. A helpful means of becoming a mindful eater is to sit down before each meal and think about what you're going to eat. Plan what is going on your plate before you have the food in front of you and don't eat more than you initially planned to until you've finished your first plate, given it some time, and determined that you really do want more food. There isn't a problem with taking more food when you need it, particularly if you've had a longer or more physically demanding day than is typical for you. Just make sure that you're doing it because you need it and not because you want to eat.

Mindful eating cuts down on a lot of those boredom cravings. Have you ever ended up in front of the refrigerator with the door open, looking at all the ingredients for something to jump out at you when you're not even really hungry? Try asking yourself the next time you're looking in the refrigerator between meals, "Am I hungry right now? Or do I just wish I had something to snack on?" If it's the latter, find something to do that will occupy your mind and take it off food. If that doesn't help, consider chewing some gum to give you a little bit of variety and flavor without all those calories.

Scheduling Your Meals

Many people don't know that your body thrives off of having a schedule. The more predictable your schedule is, the happier your body is. If you eat at the same times every day, you're going to be able to digest more effectively. If you go to sleep at the same time every day, you're going to have an easier time falling asleep and you might even find that your body naturally starts to wake up at the right time. If you exercise at the same time each day, you might find that you have an extra burst of energy at that time of day to help you get through that workout. Your body is a well-oiled machine that thrives off of a great diet, adequate sleep, and healthy amounts of activity. With these things, keeping yourself feeling your best is so much easier. This is why eating, sleeping, and exercising on a schedule is so ideal. Of course, everyone is different and if you try this and find that it doesn't quite work for you, then something else might be a better answer for you.

If you want to schedule your meals, look at an average day for you. If you wake up at 6 AM and you go to bed at 10 PM, then you have a lot of time in between to fit in your meals. You also have 8 hours allocated for sleep, which is ideal as well! You may even find that you don't need a full eight hours, which gives you some more time to play around with in your day!

So when you wake up at 6 AM, you could take that time to freshen up or maybe exercise and schedule your breakfast for about 7 or 8 in the morning. From there, you will head off to work and keep yourself nice and busy for the next 4 to 5 hours. At 12 or 1 in the afternoon, you'll have a lunch that is filled with lots of healthy and delicious nutrients and head back to the grind. Another 5 to 6 hours will go by and then it's time for a healthy, hearty dinner. That's 3 square meals a day and a great time bracket for your body to keep to. Skipping meals sometimes without any sort of reliable schedule can throw off your body and it can even keep you from consistently losing weight, so be careful.

You can certainly work some snacks in the mix here if you know that you tend to get a little bit hungry between meals, but try to schedule those as best you can, too! Doing so will allow your body to be ready for them.

Now, you might be wondering what I mean when I talk about your body being ready to digest things. Your digestive process is fairly complex and requires a number of substances in your body to happen properly. Your body must create those enzymes, chemicals, and other substances in order to complete the digestive process. If your body anticipates a meal but you don't get it, you have those substances built up and nowhere for them to go. Alternatively, if your body doesn't know a meal is coming and you eat something, your body has to put everything on hold while it generates those things to break that food down, making your digestive process take a little bit longer. Neither of these outcomes is ideal.

Planning your meals and insisting that your body get the food it needs at the same time each day can help you to maximize your metabolism potential, get food digested in record time, and keep your body from holding onto things that it doesn't need. After all, isn't all of this about getting rid of the things that your body doesn't need?

Holding Yourself Accountable

Please don't run away screaming just yet. I want to start out by saying that the accountability that we are looking for here is not the kind that you may be trying with yourself at the moment. "Accountability" can sound like such a loaded term that is filled with a lot of icky feelings, but it's actually a really simple concept that you can harness for your own empowerment.

Accountability means taking all the guilt out of your statements. Rather than having to hide the fact that you ate something that doesn't quite fall in line with your plans for your health, you own it. You say outright, "I ate that," and then you take any steps that you need to take in order to make it right.

Being accountable means that the mistakes aren't going unnoticed and that you're taking the right steps to make all of your efforts count. There are some things that you can do each day to keep yourself on top of everything that pertains to your weight loss goals. Mindful eating is a great first step, so this could be considered the next step.

Keep your food journal religiously.
Make it a point to write down each of the things that you eat throughout the day. Having to write them down and see that written list of items that you've had during the day will help to put them in perspective for you. It's possible to have long days and sometimes we forget how much we've eaten and simply go back for more whenever the mood strikes us.

Say for instance, you're working from home and you grab a little snack right after breakfast while you're working. You keep on working for a couple more hours, get completely sucked into it and forget you even had that first snack. If you write it down, you can take a look at your journal and think, "Well if I have a snack now, I won't be able to have on later. I should hold off for just a couple more hours because then it will be lunch time." Doing that can go a long way to cut down on the calories.

Even if you do go a little bit off the course with your eating for the day, having a record of it will allow you to make better choices in the following day. Making better choices, more often, over a longer period of time is exactly what will yield the most positive results in your weight loss endeavors.

Make your personal mission statement.
Your personal mission statement is one sentence that adequately sums up your overall goals. One phrase that tells the world, "this is what I'm looking to achieve and why," will allow you to conduct yourself in a coordinated manner toward that goal. Having that statement in and of itself is a step in the right direction toward those goals, but you will need to do more than just write it once in the beginning. Put it somewhere you can see it often and try to think with it when you make your choices throughout each day.

"I am going on a walk today because it falls in line with my mission statement," or "I don't want to eat this because it doesn't align with my mission statement." These are things that you should be thinking or saying when you're going through your day.

If you're the cynical type like I was when I first began my weight loss journey, you might be thinking that this is all just a little too formal. It might be, but it's also incredibly effective and if a little bit of formality is what it takes for you to achieve your goals and to have the health and weight that you want, then it's worth it. Get formal, get weird, get a little out there. Being stuck in your ways, being informal, and going with the flow of life has led you to this book, so now it's time to change things up and get a new, better result.

Reward yourself when you accomplish something.
Having goals and benchmarks along your weight loss journey can give you little wins that keep you moving on your way toward overall success. Set those goals for yourself and avidly work toward them. You will find that checking those off the list over time will give you a deeply satisfying feeling and will grease the wheels, so to speak. When you reach these little benchmarks that you make for yourself, it's a great idea to reward yourself in a way that is meaningful to you.

Consider some things that you enjoy or things that make you happy and make a sturdy promise to yourself to get them when you meet your goals. If you felt like going the extra mile, you could even hold littler ceremonies for yourself. Make little award cards for yourself and bestow them upon yourself along with the reward that you've chosen and really make a big deal out of it.

You might feel silly the first time, but it's something exciting to look forward to and to build on. People often thrive when they're given the space to be creative and to put their own flair into something. Give yourself the space to come up with creative, unique, and gratifying rewards for reaching those benchmarks and really spoil yourself when you meet them!

The biggest piece of advice I will give you here is that you should try to avoid making food a part of the plan for rewards.

You are worth more than snacks, so pick a reward that reflects you and your personality and get yourself something or do something for yourself that you wouldn't normally do like getting a massage or going out to a movie.

Celebrate the little things.
Weight loss is about the long haul. You're going to be focusing on your weight loss for a while until you're able to get yourself down to that ideal number, which is going to take some time. Remember, slow and steady wins the race. Just as I mentioned above, setting benchmarks and goals for yourself is a great way to keep yourself focused and motivated to move toward your goal.

In addition to this, pay close attention to the things that you struggle with in the beginning and think about all the things that you'd like to improve. For instance, if you think that you would like to drink fewer carbonated drinks throughout the week, put them in your food journal along with everything that you've been eating and keep tabs on it while trying to bring your consumption down a little bit. When you hit a new low number each week, take some time to celebrate! Do a little bit of an activity that you enjoy to celebrate and concentrate on just doing better and better as time goes on!

Chapter 4: The 4 Golden Rules of Eating

There are some rules that you can follow when you're trying to make good choices for your health that might just keep you from getting too bogged down in the minutia. There are so many different things you can do to lose weight and there are so many tips and tricks for you to follow. It can help to have some basic core rules to follow in the beginning that give you a strong basis to work off of, then you can go from there and built on the things that you find work for you over time and as you get more comfortable. Let's cover those basics now.

When You Are Hungry, Eat

It can be hard to get caught up in the scheduling and in the menu planning. You can plan everything out so thoroughly and end up missing the point: you're supposed to eat when you're hungry. This doesn't mean you have to wait until the pains start and it doesn't mean that you should be eating all the time, either. If you sense hunger in your body, have a moderate portion of food to resolve that.

For some people, learning to be healthy and learning to eat in a health-conscious manner means learning what it really feels like when you're getting hungry and what it feels like when your body is telling you that it wants a little something more than it needs. Gauging those impulses and the differences between them can really be a lifesaver in the long run.

So, without too much fuss or fluff: if you are hungry, eat.

Eat What You Want, Not What You Think You Should Have

As you continue to adjust to your regimen, you will start to be able to trust more of your inclinations when it comes to foods.

You will get more and more comfortable coming up with meal plans that are made up of foods that you want to eat, rather than the foods that you think your diet should contain. Now, this might come off as a little bit confusing, so I'll elaborate.

You will want to make sure that the foods you eat are not too far off the rails for a meal. You will also want to make sure that you're not going for foods that bring you absolutely no joy. Say no to salads with no dressing, no flavor, no meat, and no substance. Pick salads with meat, egg, herbs, delicious dressings, and plenty of flavor.

Don't settle for a dry slab of baked chicken with a frozen vegetable medley and plain brown rice if that's not what you want. Have stews made with wholesome and fresh ingredients. Make delicious burrito bowls at home. Have amazing sashimi with a little bit of rice if you want it. Don't settle!

Eat Consciously and Enjoy Every Mouthful

This is what we talked about before with being mindful of the things that you eat. Be mindful when you eat and make sure you really take the time and attention to enjoy the things that you're eating at every meal. Doing so will make your meals more interesting, more rewarding, and it will help you to feel more full by the end of each meal.

Make sure that you're eating on purpose, not out of habit. Make sure that you're enjoying what you're eating because you've put lots of good, naturally bold and delicious flavors into your food.

You may need to practice being mindful when you're eating, but that's not a problem. Just keep trying until you get comfortable with it!

When You Think You Are Full, Stop Eating

This might seem like a no-brainer to some people. Do not eat past the point of being full, or you will usually regret it. This is where eating mindfully and taking your time can really come in handy. Some of us will eat without our minds on what we're doing and we will eat so quickly that we pass the point of being full without even realizing it.

If you're eating slowly and mindfully, your stomach will get to send the signal to your brain that it has had enough and it is up to you from there to listen to that signal, put the remainder of your food away for a later time, and not pick it up again until you're in need of more food.

Over time, you will find it easier and easier to know when you've had enough food and you won't even think about going past that point unless it's a special occasion or the food is so good you can't stop. Hopefully those occurrences are rare, though!

Chapter 5: Practical Weight Loss Advice

A lot of this book is focused on the mental power that food can have over our minds and thus, causing serious weight gain and other health issues. **Please, do not underestimate the power that your mind has over either your ability or inability to lose weight.** If you question this, then it could affect the success that you will find in this book. Not recognizing the importance of managing and changing your thoughts around food, working out, and nutrition will ignore the core problem of your eating issues.

Having said that, I wanted to dedicate this chapter to practical weight loss advice. As well as including 50 health-focused recipes in this book, this chapter will go through some practical tips on losing weight that you may or may not have considered before.

Intermittent Fasting:

I want to cover intermittent fasting for a number of reasons. One, intermittent fasting is not a diet. It is a lifestyle change. Throughout this book, we are focusing on lifestyle changes as opposed to yoyo diets. Intermittent fasting is also very flexible. Not only does it offer many different types of fasting, but it can also mold into your day-to-day schedule easily. There have been countless medical and scientific reports on the benefit of this style of eating. Typically, everyone should be having a 12-hour gap between when they omit food. This is so that our food can be properly digested and our body has a chance to go into **ketosis**.

What is ketosis?

Ketosis is a molecular process that happens when your body is starved of carbohydrates to burn for energy. Since there are no carbs available, instead, it burns fat and creates ketones which it can use for fuel. Intermittent fasting is when ketosis naturally occurs due to you elongating the hours of which you eat. This means that by creating a bigger gap between when you eat and when you don't, you are naturally allowing your body to burn fat, without having to actually skip a meal. Many people enjoy a normal, nutritious diet with intermittent fasting. In fact, under-eating when intermittent fasting is not advised. This can actually have a negative effect on your metabolism, slowing it down. That being said, it is also very important not to overeat when fasting, thus eliminating the positive weight loss results that you have obtained in your fasting window. The recipes that have been written in this book will serve as a great guideline in what to eat whilst intermittent fasting.

Intermittent Fasting:

Intermittent fasting is the irregular or inconsistent act of fasting for short periods of time to gain optimal effect. This could include alternate-day fasting, daily time-restricted feeding, and periodic fasting, all of which have weight loss and health benefits. If fasting is something that is new to you, then intermittent fasting is a great place to start. Not only can you do it gradually, but it shouldn't put your body under any kind of hunger shock. You can choose a style that compliments your daily tasks and one that works around your schedule, instead of *you* working around *it*!

Intermittent fasting simply elongates the hours during which you fast, or stop eating, by scheduling when you eat, as opposed to worrying so much about what you eat. Let's take a look at the different methods of doing this:

- Leangains protocol - aka the 16/8 method. Fasting for 16 hours and restricting your eating period to 8 hours. This usually involves not eating breakfast and instead, having your first meal at 12 pm for example, with your last meal being at 8 pm. Fairly simple, right?

- The 5:2 diet - This type of intermittent fasting can vary from consuming a smaller amount of calories, two days out of the week (not side-by-side), and eating as you normally would on the remaining five days out of the week. The smaller calorie intake would usually range from 500-600 calories.

- Eat-Stop-Eat diet - This is a style of fasting where you fast for a full 24 hours, once or twice a week. Let's imagine that you eat dinner on Tuesday evening at 7 pm. If you are fasting the eat-stop-eat way, then you will not eat until Wednesday evening at 7 pm. You may only want to do this once a week when starting off, as it can take the body time to adjust to a day without food, especially around lunchtime. Of course, you can always try to implement this habit gradually and work your way up to fasting for 24 hours at one time.

Whether you are fasting once a week, controlling the periods in which you eat again, or if you choose to reduce calorie intake two days out of seven, these are all beneficial in their own right and can be considered healthy practices of intermittent fasting. Let's take a closer look at the three listed types of intermittent fasting, and what you should consider about each.

Weight Loss:
Weight loss becomes much less about "looks" when we are older and much more about "management." Perhaps you have bought this book because your doctor has suggested that you try to lose weight in a healthy manner, in order to

maintain your health as you reach this next stage in your life. Or perhaps you are looking for a lifestyle change, as opposed to a diet, that doesn't involve sacrificing the things that you enjoy in life, such as a good steak or a glass of wine. For me, this is an essential detail about intermittent fasting that makes it so appealing. Elongating the time that I fast means that I savor and really enjoy my eating window a lot more. It has also allowed me to be that bit more conscious about what I consume during eating hours. So, do you need to skip breakfast in order to benefit from the weight loss effects of intermittent fasting? The short answer is no, you don't. Many people decide to eat three meals within their allocated eating period and still manage to lose weight. There is no need to restrict when you are eating and intermittent fasting. Your body is doing work behind the scenes that you are not even aware of. Essentially, the way that intermittent fasting works is by the body being induced into a ketogenic state. Ketosis is a metabolic state whereby the body has a high concentration of ketones in the blood. This occurs when fat is providing the majority of fuel for the body, and there is limited access to glucose. Glucose, better known as blood sugar, is low, allowing the body to go to the fat cells for energy. The University School of Medicine in Atlanta states that "intermittent fasting induces a ketogenic state, as evidenced by the rise in β-hydroxybutyrate levels in overweight individuals who fast. After 6–8 hours of fasting, ketone levels become detectable, which signals a switch from fat storage to fat utilization with a decrease in low-density lipoproteins (LDL) and an increase in high-density lipoproteins (HDL) levels. This change from using glucose as energy to using fatty acids and ketones for energy is called intermittent metabolic switching. Furthermore, the ketogenic diet promotes weight loss, as processing ketones requires greater energy." (Am J Med, Aug 20) This explains how people can lose weight while fasting without having to restrict their diet during their eating windows. By delaying the hours that we fast and elongating them, the body enters ketosis, which promotes weight loss, to put it more simply. One study cited in the paper found that overweight men with type II diabetes who were either participating in caloric restriction or intermittent fasting regimens experienced weight loss, with the intermittent fasting subjects losing 1.1% of body fat with a mean 6.5% weight loss after 12 weeks. The study states that similar findings were observed in both overweight and obese premenopausal females who were randomized to intermittent fasting and caloric restriction for 6 months. (Am J Med, Aug 20) Interestingly, the intermittent fasting and caloric restriction groups had comparable results with the intermittent fasting group losing 6.4 kilograms, and the caloric restriction group losing 5.6 kilograms. (Am J Med, Aug 20)

This is encouraging for those who may have been dreading the idea of restricting and dieting as part of their lifestyle change. It is true that it can take people and also our bodies a certain amount of time to get used to fasting. Our bodies really appreciate and thrive off of routine and a predictable eating schedule. So naturally, if you maintain a fasting habit for a number of weeks or months, such as the subjects referenced in the above study, then not only should you see a reduction in body mass, but your body will also get used to it. As you start to practice and then maintain the habit of intermittent fasting, your body will get much more used to eating within a selected period. The studies referenced essentially show that it is possible to maintain an enjoyable lifestyle and diet while losing weight. While this is true, it is important not to *over*eat during your eating windows. If you are eating more in your eating window than you would have before, then the weight loss will not be as evident, and your body will balance out and stay the way it is. It is equally important not to *under*eat during your eating window. If you have ever heard statements that intermittent fasting can cause people to become nutrient deficient, this is not true. Nutritional value will restore itself during your eating window, but if you are under-eating during this eating window, then your body will continue to think that you are in ketosis. This could not only lead to nutritional deficiencies, but it could also lead to a slowing down of the metabolism over time. Finding the correct balance with food during your eating windows is an important factor in finding success with intermittent fasting and weight loss.

The Warrior Diet

If you have chanted the Warrior hypnosis before reading this book, then you will love the sound of what is known as The Warrior Diet. The Warrior Diet, created in 2001, is a type of intermittent fasting that is supposed to follow the eating patterns of ancient warriors. These people ate a limited diet during the day and were free to feast at night. It is supposed to stress the body through reduced food intake, which should then trigger the "survival instincts" that allow people to reduce their diet.

However, keep in mind that this diet is based on observations and beliefs of the creator, Ori Hofmekler, who is a former member of the Israeli Special Forces. He experienced this during his career and took it with him as he transitioned to fitness and nutrition.

During this diet, you are expected to undereat for 20 hours each day, and then eat during a four-hour period at night, consuming as much as you care to do so. During the fasting period, you can consume a small amount of dairy, raw fruits and veggies, or hard boiled eggs. Then, during the 4-hour eating period, you can binge on anything that you want, with emphasis on healthy and organic foods.

This diet requires a three-week plan that can be divided into phases:

- **Phase I:** The first week is a week of detox. This involves undereating during the day, only consuming vegetable juice, clear broth, dairy, hard-boiled eggs, or fruits and veggies that are raw and unprocessed. During the eating period, you can have a salad with vinegar and oil dressing, and one or more meals with plant proteins, wheat-free grains, small amounts of cheese, and cooked veggies. During the day, you can have coffee, tea, or water.
- **Phase II:** During the second week, you boost the amount of fat you consume. This involves undereating for 20 hours during the day with veggie juices, clear broth, dairy, hard-boiled eggs, or raw fruits and veggies. During the eating period, you may have a salad with oil and vinegar. Then, you can have lean animal protein, cooked veggies, and then consume at least one handful of nuts. Do not consume any starches or grains during this time.
- **Phase III:** During the third week, you conclude fat loss. This involves cycling between high-carb and high-protein intake. There should be 1-2 days of high-carb eating, 1-2 days of high-protein and low carb eating, 1-2 days of high-carb eating, and 1-2 days of high protein, low-carb eating.
    - High-carb days involve undereating for 20 hours, eating only veggie juices, clear broth, dairy, hard-boiled eggs, and raw fruits and veggies. During the eating period, you may have a salad with oil and vinegar, cooked veggies, a small amount of animal protein, and one primary form of carbohydrate.
    - High-protein days involve undereating with the same foods dictated previously. Then, during the four-hour overeating period, you may have a salad with oil and vinegar, 816 ounces of protein, and a side of non-starchy veggies, preferably cooked. Do not consume

grains or starches during this period, but you can enjoy fresh tropical fruit for dessert if you want to.

Once all three weeks have been completed, the stages can be started over and cycled again. Or, if you want to, you can forgo the phases and start undereating for 20 hours, then eating healthy, protein-rich meals during the overeating phases. As you follow this diet, there are no specific caloric limits. However, it is recommended that you supplement with a multivitamin, probiotics, and amino acids. During this time, it's recommended for you to also incorporate exercise and hydration. You want to make sure that you have plenty of hydration when restricting your eating, especially because you do get a lot of water from your diet. Foods like watermelon, greens, and other plants are full of water that helps to keep you hydrated.

Keto, Plant-Based, and Other Diets:

If you live in a major city, then you probably have a good idea of the many diet trends that are active in modern society right now. Whether it is a keto restaurant serving coffee with butter, a plant-based burger joint, or an Italian restaurant that boasts about gluten-free pizza, it can be a little overwhelming considering which one of these options may help us on our weight loss journey, and which ones should be avoided.

Harvard University's food chart states the following: eat a large selection of leafy greens, vegetables, white fish, poultry, and some small animal fats, sparingly eat red meat, and avoid foods such as bacon and deli meats.

When I reread this paper recently, I was surprised to find that those deli meats and bacon should be avoided entirely. But then I reminded myself about the importance of balance. Is it a big problem if I order some bacon in a restaurant every once in a while? No. Does that mean that I should store a couple of packets in my fridge, to have at my disposal any time I want? Also no. If you have tempting foods in your life, start first by simply reading the back of the labels.

As a non-drinker, I always opt for Tonic Water and lime juice. In fact, I like to enjoy two-three of these drinks every evening. Until recently, when I looked at a 100ml bottle, which had a whopping 33 grams of sugar inside! This product should not be considered water, it is anything but!

Since then, I now use tonic water as a treat and switched to sparkling water and lime instead. It still refreshes me and gives me that same satisfaction, but I have reduced my sugar intake a huge amount.

Whatever diet may interest you, you must ensure that you are reading the back of labels. Very often, foods that are marketed as "low fat", "gluten-free", or "zero" can have a ton of hidden additives and replacements that are less than healthy. If you have been living off of low-fat and calorie-friendly frozen meals, and have not been able to see a positive improvement, it may be due to what you are eating.

This is why I have made a point of including a lot of healthy recipes at the end of this book. The most empowering thing for someone who struggles with their weight is putting that control back into your own hands. If you aren't a fan of cooking, **question that negativity bias!** You may soon learn that going to the kitchen after a long day and listening to your favorite music while cooking something delicious distracts you from wanting to binge eat or order takeout. Do you fancy something sweet? Great! Why not choose one of the health-conscious recipes in this book instead of allowing yourself to buy a large chocolate bar from the store? Baking, again, gives the control back into your hands. You know exactly how much sugar has been put into it and you can save the treats for each day, preparing yourself for success.

Chapter 6: Making Way for Progress

Doing a little bit of prep work before your diet and your weight loss endeavors can go a long way. There are some things that can just trip you up a little bit and keep you from getting the most out of your weight loss regimen and we'll address those here so you can set yourself up for the best possible success.

Prepare Your Kitchen

Doing a little bit of prep work in your kitchen can keep you from having those fights with yourself about what you should and shouldn't be eating. Sometimes when you're working on losing weight and you're trying to be more conscious of what you eat, you will find that you're looking for something that doesn't quite fall in line with your goals or with your meal plans for the week. If you have something that doesn't fall into those plans in your house and you find yourself in that mode, you will eat it.

Setting yourself up by success by preparing your kitchen could mean going through the pantry, the freezer, the refrigerator, and any other places where you keep food and snacks and doing away with what you have there. You don't necessarily have to throw it away, but keeping it around if you never intend to eat it is just as wasteful. Unless you secretly plan to eat it at some point, which is setting yourself up for a bit of backslide in your goals. You could gift it to a friend if you are concerned with food waste. You could also let a family member have it, but only *if that family member doesn't live in your house and share your kitchen*, because then the food hasn't really gone anywhere.

Another way you will want to prepare your kitchen is by making sure that you have any appliances, storage, or tools that you might need. If you're going to be prepping meals for yourself, you want to make sure that you have enough containers, a good cutting board, some knives, the right cookware, and anything that you might not have. Sure, it's rare to be setting up a kitchen for the first time while also overhauling everything that you eat at the same time, but these things do happen and I want to make sure that every reader is accommodated in the advice given here.

Take yourself through your meal plan and exactly how you would prepare and store all of it so you can be sure you have everything you need. Over time, you can acquire more things that you might need, but so long as you have enough to get you through the first few meal plans, you should be good as gold!

Your kitchen should be well-stocked with the things that you like to eat that are good for you. If you enjoy snacking on sliced bell peppers, make sure you have plenty of those in your kitchen. If you love to have eggs in the morning, make sure you have plenty at the beginning of your week. If you love to have some fresh fruit throughout your day, make sure that's in your kitchen as well. Anything that you feel you will want to eat throughout the week, make sure it's in your kitchen. If it's not in your kitchen, you have to go get it and that introduces opportunities for you to veer off the path you've set for yourself and do things that you might not have planned to do in the beginning.

Take a little bit of time to think about some of the sweeter things that you would like to have in your diet as well. Keep a little bit of that in your kitchen so you're able to indulge a little bit from time to time throughout your week. If you're used to dessert, you might need a little bit of something sweet after dinner to help you acclimate to your new lifestyle.

Prepare Your Mind

Being on a diet and trying to lose weight is so much harder when you're not mentally prepared for it. If you're stuck thinking that you're only going to be on this diet for a little while until you're ready to get back to your regular means of eating, then you might find it hard to stick it out for the long haul. This can also happen when you're stuck thinking that the diet is some kind of punishment for something.

Being on a healthy food regimen is not something that should make you feel guilt or shame in your everyday routine. It's something that should help you to feel your best and that should give you a guideline for how to plan your meals and plan your days. It is something that should, over time, make you feel more healthy, more confident, and more able to achieve your health and fitness goals.

By preparing yourself for your new fitness and health regimen, you're opening yourself up to the changes that should come from it. You're allowing yourself to receive the help that such changes can give you. Believe it or not, being closed off to it can sabotage your progress!

Make sure that you have your head on straight about your regimen and if you have questions about how you're supposed to get through the day-to-day, get those answered before you get started. Going into a new regimen with a hefty dose of uncertainty can also trip you up over time.

The best idea is to fully understand everything about your weight loss regimen, be confident in its ability to help you, and to remain gung ho about making that regimen work for you. Throw yourself into it and really invest your time and energy into making that regimen work for you, because it's something that is important to you, it's something that matters, and it's something that will help you in the long run.

There might be a little bit of a bumpy start, but with mental prep, you can get over that hurdle without too much trouble. We'll cover more about expectation management in a later section in this chapter.

Prepare Your Journal

You will be shocked to learn how much a journal has to do with weight loss and fitness. Now, there are actually a couple of journals to which I'm referring here. The first one we're going to cover is your food journal.

I've mentioned that writing down your food and documenting all the things that you intake can help you with accountability. It can also help you to get a really good handle on what you're taking in, what you're putting out (calorie-wise), and how you can amend to make improvements in your weight loss.

You don't need to journal your food forever, but doing it at the outset is a great way for you to understand how it's supposed to look. Now, when you're first getting started and you're trying to prepare for your new regimen, you can start journaling before you ever change any of your eating habits. Doing this can have a couple of benefits.

The first benefit to this is that you can see how much you have really been eating without paying attention to it. You can see what mistakes you've been making potentially without even realizing it, and you can see how much that all adds up to each day. If it's more than 2,000 calories, that could answer any questions you have about where any excess weight could be coming from depending on your activity level.

The second benefit is that you can get used to the concept of logging each and every thing you eat throughout the day. In the very beginning, this can seem like a real chore, so getting used to it before you ever even touch the diet can help you to maintain that habit while so many other habits are changing around it.

The next kind of journal is a mental one. When you change your diet and your activity patterns, you will be going through a lot, whether you feel like it or not. Your body will be changing a lot of the things about the way it operates, you will be changing a lot of things about what you can expect from your whole day, and you start to see the ways in which food was supporting you, if any. There are quite a few people who give up their food crutches without even realizing it, then it feels like the whole world dropped out from under them out of nowhere.

If you're going to be doing self-hypnosis, you're going to be dealing with your subconscious mind and you're going to be working to replace some of those conclusions and imposed thoughts that you don't consciously believe or even see. This can stir things up a bit and it can cause some difficulty emotionally and mentally. It's important when you feel these types of disruptions, to write them down, to journal them, and to work through them as best you can.

These things will often not stick around when you continue to work through them with your self-hypnosis. They might just pass through, but it's important to keep yourself on the lookout for these types of things and to have a place to write it all down, get it all out, put it into words, and see what it looks like down on the page.

You may find that you don't really need that kind of support, but it's best to give yourself that avenue. Better to have it and not need it than to need it and not have it, right?

So much about this regimen and these processes is about keeping your state of mind healthy, about keeping your relationship with yourself and food on healthy terms. Talking through everything and being able to sort through the ideas that are consciously your own and the ideas that are more of a subconscious thought of unknown origin can be immensely helpful to you.

Keep that journal handy and make sure you say everything that you need to say.

Prepare Your Loved Ones

The people around us have become just as accustomed to our habits as we have. They are used to seeing us do certain things, they're used to seeing us reach for certain things, and they're used to the things that we typically do to make ourselves feel better. This can often lead to them trying to help you get through your harder days with the foods and coping mechanisms that you once used to get you through those moments.

It can be a good idea to look through those mechanisms and behaviors that your partner, friends, or loved ones might have picked up on and tell them which ones you're intent on changing. "No more chocolate for my birthday," is one that you might want to cover. "Don't take me out to dinner to celebrate things anymore," "I don't want to order out when I've had a bad day anymore," or even "Let's stay away from food-themed gifts."

Your loved ones might have a hard time adjusting to this, but making sure that they know about these things is a good first step. Together, you can work to move past them and phase out those habits, traditions, and things that have become normal over time.

If you need a little bit of extra support from the loved ones who share your home with you, it could be helpful to make sure they know as much about your new regimen as possible so they can try to follow it along with you if they feel so inclined. If they're willing to do this, you won't be faced with those foods that you can't have nearly as often and you might be more inclined to stick with your diet when you don't have to watch those closest to you enjoy the foods that you wish you could be eating right along with them.

Manage Expectations

Expectations can be a heck of a thing to have to wrestle when you're already going through the troubles of going through such dramatic changes. Particularly with something like weight loss, which can take a long time depending on what you've got to lose, it can be hard to maintain focus, drive, confidence, inspiration, motivation, and positivity. If you feel like you should be making a certain amount of progress each week and you're not making that progress, it can be a significant mental drawback that makes you feel like maybe it's not worth it to be spending so much time and effort on these goals.

Before I say anything else, let me assure you *it is* **absolutely** *worth so much time and effort* to work toward these goals. The next thing I want to make sure you know is that *progress is **not** a straight line.* Progress has setbacks, relapses, difficulties, obstacles, curveballs, and so much more that can make you feel like you're going in the wrong direction. So long as you have your eyes on that prize and so long as you're working hard to stay on the regimen, you're going in the right direction.

Remind yourself that you will not lose a pound every single day. Remind yourself that you might even have some weeks where you don't lose at all. Remind yourself that these things do not mean that you're not doing everything correctly. There are so many indicators of a healthy diet, a healthy lifestyle, and a healthy relationship with food and your body.

Make sure that you're looking at the clarity of your skin, the quality of your sleep, the way you feel, your energy level, your outlook about yourself, your outlook about food, how you feel about the diet you've made for yourself, how you feel about the things you get to do differently now, and how things have changed for the better since you've adopted this way of living. When you take all of that into account, make sure that you're not just using the number on the scale to completely overshadow all of those other factors.

You're in this for the long haul and you need to make sure that your expectations reflect that!

Chapter 7: More on Self-Hypnosis

Relax Completely - The Progressive Technique

The first step in self-hypnosis is to relax completely. Put yourself in a position that will allow you to relax the most. Sit in a comfortable chair, sit in a comfortable position on the floor, or lie down.

For some, the concept of relaxing comes very naturally. It's just a matter of thinking, *relax* and all the muscles just go along with the plan and all the tension is just gone all at once. For many others, however, relaxing takes a bit of doing, which I know sounds counterintuitive.

There are many ways in which you can fully relax your body, but I'll explain a nice basic method here that you can use to get you restarted. You are always encouraged to look into methods and find something that better fits your needs. The more tailored to you the self-hypnosis routine is, the better results you will get from it.

Place yourself in a chair, on the floor, or lying down and close your eyes. Put your concentration on the very top of your head and feel the muscles there. Relax them completely. Very, very slowly, concentrate on the muscles in the zones of your body moving from the top of your head, all the way down to your toes, and relax each of them one by one. When you get to the bottoms of your feet, you should be completely relaxed.

If you feel more tension that creeped up on you while you were working on those muscles, start back at the top and do another sweep downward to relax them once again. When you have fully relaxed all the muscles in your body, you will be ready to start with your self-hypnosis.

Relax Completely - The Confusional Technique

If you're not sure if the technique above would work for you or if you're simply looking for another technique, there is one called confusional technique. This is when you give yourself a task that might seem rather odd to you that will completely occupy your mind and allow you to relax your entire body. This one might take some getting used to before you fully feel at ease using it. Try it out a couple of times and see if it works to put you completely at ease.

In a space that you've created for yourself to fully relax, seat or lie yourself comfortably. From there, close your eyes, do your best to release the tension from your body, then count backwards from 100, closing your eyes on the odd numbers and opening them on the even ones.

This occupies your mind with those thoughts and puts the concentration in blinking on purpose, taking control of an impulse that normally keeps itself moving on its own. Doing this can help to bring your body to a state of relaxation.

If you find that you tense up when keeping tabs on your counting and your blinking, consider using the progressive technique or other relaxation techniques that will allow you to get into the right mindset and mode of relaxation for self-hypnosis.

Finding Your Method

Finding the right method for you when it comes to self-hypnosis can take a couple of tries. Don't get discouraged if you try a couple of different things and don't find something that immediately works for you. It's important to remember that you're not trying to put yourself out of consciousness when you're self-hypnotizing. Here are some things to remember that you are ***not*** trying to achieve when you're doing self-hypnosis.

Brain-washing or mind control
It is a mistake to think in the beginning of your self-hypnosis that you're going to be changing your whole outlook to some other mode that isn't healthy. Hypnosis isn't something that should be used in an attempt to make other people do things they wouldn't normally do of their own volition.
Trying to take control of someone's mental state and impose conclusions, thought processes, beliefs, or other things on them is not something achievable through proper hypnosis and it's not something that ought to be attempted by any means.
You don't need to be worry that any of the methods you choose for self-hypnosis will impose anything on you that doesn't ring true for you or serve you properly.

Sleep or unconsciousness
If you notice that you're falling asleep when you're doing your relaxation in the beginning of your self-hypnosis, take a moment to wake yourself up, shake off those sleepies, invigorate yourself, and then get back to it. If you haven't slept enough the night before your hypnosis and you find yourself unable to stay awake for it, try again on a day when you have gotten an adequate amount of sleep. You might not even realize that you're tired enough to doze off until you're completely relaxed. Just keep an eye out and adjust as you need to.

A higher state of consciousness or some mystical level of spirituality
Self-hypnosis isn't a gateway to a higher state of consciousness like meditation or other practices that might, on the surface, seem similar in nature to self-hypnosis. Self-hypnosis is not about elevating your consciousness or putting you in touch with the universe. It's solely about putting positive statements and affirmations into your subconscious mind so you can give yourself a head-start on your goals in life. In the specific case of this book, we are going to be using it to overwrite some of

the negative things that could be holding you back from reaching your true potential.

A strange new state or altered state
One of the things I want to be abundantly clear about when it comes to self-hypnosis. You are not trying to change anything about who you are or how you think on a basic level. You are simply putting affirmations and positive thoughts into your subconscious that open up your ability to achieve the things you might be holding yourself back from achieving.
If you're hoping to change your mode of thinking or shift into a different personality, you're looking in the wrong place. When you are through with your hypnosis, you're still going to be yourself, you're still going to think like you, and you're still going to hold the same values. Changing who you are isn't something you'll get with self-hypnosis.

When you are looking for the ideal method for you, you want to find something that makes you comfortable and which speaks to you. If you are skeptical of it or if you are trying to convince yourself that it will work, you're going to be too hung up on those things for you to really gain the benefits of the powerful technique you're engaged in. You want to make sure that you're finding the right things in your method. Here are some of the things you ***are*** looking for in your self-hypnosis regimen:

Relaxation that is total and complete throughout your body and your mind.
Put yourself into a place where you can enjoy the atmosphere, where you can be physically comfortable, and orient your body in such a way that you can relax all your muscles without causing yourself problems when it's time to get up. Get totally comfortable and allow your body to release the tensions of the day, to let go of any grumpiness or stress that it might be retaining for the moment, and just give yourself over to the process.

Affirmations, words, phrases, and suggestions that make sense to you and which strike a chord with you.
If you are trying to use overly flowery sayings because they are what you think someone else would want you to be using for your self-hypnosis regimen, then you are starting out on a bad foot. These suggestions have to make sense to you and to resonate with you because you have to be the one who believes them. Your subconscious mind is tucking these suggestions away to be used just beneath your awareness to help you continue on through your life. If you pick phrases you don't believe, they will not stick.

A genuine sense of self discovery and understanding.
Take an interest in yourself. Take an interest in your own mind, your own problems, your own solutions, your own difficulties, and your own triumphs. Realize that you have everything to do with each one of those things, that you are not on the receiving end of anything and that you are the one who puts everything in your life into play from here on out. Invest in your mental health and you will get out of it exactly what you're putting into it. Put forth the effort to understand, know about, and care for yourself and you will find your therapy will go so much faster than if you were simply a passenger along for the ride.

Getting Started

1. In order to begin this process, you're going to have to feel absolutely relaxed and comfortable. Using the techniques in the section above can help you to achieve this.
2. Find a focal point in the room that you can watch while you're doing this process. Looking slightly upward and out from yourself is an ideal way to go, like a piece of wall art.
3. Purge your mind of any and all thoughts and simply put all of your focus onto the object in the room that you have chosen.

4. Put your attention (without shifting your gaze) on your own eyes. Think about the movements of your eyelids and feel them becoming heavy as you relax and feel them closing slowly. Put some attention then on your breathing and keep your breathing slow and even.
5. Each time you breathe out, try to focus on relaxing even more than you already were a moment before. This may feel impossible, but you may surprise yourself.
6. In your mind's eye, envision an object moving rhythmically either up and down or side to side. A metronome, a grandfather clock pendulum, a bouncing ball, whatever imagery you choose. Focus on that slow and steady movement with your mind's eye.
7. In your head, count slowly backwards from 10 in a monotone and repeat "I am relaxing" in between each number. 10. I am relaxing. 9. I am relaxing. 8… and so on.
8. Once you get to the end of your counting, believe that you have reached your hypnotic state and tell yourself that you have achieved that.
9. This is the point where you will focus on your personal statements. Take the affirmations, suggestions, or statements that you have chosen and recite them to yourself here. Repeat this statement to yourself as many times as you feel is necessary and inform yourself that they are true.
10. Relax once again and allow your mind to clear of all the statements and anything that might have come up along with those. If you experienced any intrusive thoughts, kindly see them out and allow yourself to get back to your most relaxed state.
11. Take your time to slowly count to 10, but as you get higher, increase your energy with each number. In between each number, inform yourself that you will feel completely rested when you "awaken" from your hypnosis.

12. Awaken from your hypnosis and feel completely refreshed! Allow your mind to catch up with you for a couple of moments before you head out into your day or back to your daily activities, then continue on your daily routine feeling revitalized.

Finding Mantras or Statements

Choosing a mantra for your meditations is something that is deeply personal to you. The only person who can tell you what mantra will resonate with or work best for you is you. You can use these five criteria to help you to choose the right mantra for you.

It's important to make sure that your mantras are deeply personal for you, because if that mantra resonates with you, then you're going to get much more of a return on your meditation processes. Let's take a look at the five things you should bear in mind when you're using your mantra!

Use Inspirational Phrases

It is imperative that the words in your mantra speak to you on a deep level. You may not be a spiritual person, so I don't want to say that you should feel it in your soul, or that you should feel it on a spiritual level. You should absolutely feel those words resonate somewhere within you and they should inspire you to make the necessary changes in your life that will get you closer to your goal. If you're not someone who puts very much stock into flowery phrases, then pick something that has more of a pragmatic feeling to it. If you're someone who needs a little bit more flair to your mantra, then do it up!

Surrender to the Truth in It

Giving yourself over to your mantra is the next step in making it work magic in your life. Once you have picked a mantra that has really resonated with you and inspired you, you must give yourself over to it. Surrendering completely to that mantra as a complete fact will allow you to take comfort in it as a fundamental truth in your life, in the world, and in the universe. For instance, if you happen to struggle with your self worth, then you can use your mantra to state, "You have always been worthy," or something similar to this. This is a truth that you can state to yourself and to which you can surrender yourself. Once you've done that, it's no longer something you have to struggle to believe because it is simply truth.

Commit Yourself to Your Mantra
Part of making a mantra work for you is committing to it, at least for a few days. You might not get it right on the first try and you might land on a mantra that doesn't quite speak to you as well after a few days.
Committing to a mantra for at least a few days allows you to see whether or not a mantra can settle in and gain greater power and meaning for you, or whether it's a dud. It's important to develop a sort of relationship with each of your mantras so you can give yourself a chance to really find a deeper value and meaning in it before you move on to another one.

Repetition is Absolutely Key
Part and parcel to your commitment to your mantra is the repetition of it. By using your mantra at least 20 times on your first experience with it, you can really start to find the deeper meaning in it. You can start to connect it with the things that pop into your mind when you're repeating it. This pushes that mantra deeper into your mind and allows you to use it with similar situations as you live and grow.
If you find that your mind wanders away from your mantra when you're using this practice, simply explore the fine art of forgiving yourself and gently return yourself to it, then continue your repetitions.

Become One with Your Mantra
Allow yourself to meld with your mantra. To do so is to recognize the individuality of that mantra and its ability to

stand on its own as an inherent truth. That way, when the going gets tough, you and your mantra are both your own entities *as well as one single entity* and all it takes is for you to allow yourself to return to that mantra, that truth. Living your mantra will imbue it with life and allow it to come to life on its own!

Here are some sample mantras:

1. I am the solution to my problem.
2. I keep my strength for the moments when I am feeling weak.
3. The weight was not gained overnight and won't be lost overnight either.
4. If you're not hungry for healthy foods, you're probably not hungry.
5. I will be the healthiest version of me.
6. I have caused my problems and I can fix them just as easily.
7. ENOUGH!
8. There is no wagon. You are simply living.
9. Face your stuff. Don't Stuff your face.
10. I love myself beautiful, toned, and healthy. I'm happy I am mine.
11. I am not a junk human. I cannot live on junk food.
12. No matter what, keep going.
13. Failing to plan is planning to fail.
14. I am in complete control of my future.
15. I might be moving slowly, but I'm still going faster than everyone still on the couch.

Chapter 8: Hypnosis Mantras and Methods

This chapter of the book contains copies of the self-hypnosis practice. On step nine of each one, you will have the opportunity to put your own affirmations into it. Consult the list of affirmations below, then consult the approaches and see which one fits you best. Pick what lines up for you, choose your affirmations, and create your very own self-hypnosis program!

Affirmations

Losing weight is something I can easily do.
Achieving my goals brings me power.
I am losing weight with every passing day.
I love moving my body and pushing my limits.
The foods I eat each day are fuel that pushes me toward my goals.
I deserve to look and feel the way I want.
I don't eat when I don't need to.
I don't need food to cope.
I don't suffer from food cravings
I easily choose healthy foods over indulgent ones.
I enjoy pushing my body's fitness boundaries and expanding them each day.
I find exercise freeing and fulfilling.
I find it easy to be disciplined with my meals.
I have the strength to resist temptation and to spoil myself with healthy food.
I lose weight without trying.
I love moving my body to achieve my fitness goals.
I love my body and I take care of it every day.
I love my exercise regimen.

I love to snack on fruits and veggies instead of processed stuff.
I only eat when I am hungry.
Junk food doesn't bring me joy.
Living a healthy lifestyle brings me joy.
Losing weight is something that comes naturally to me.
My body is thriving.

A Pragmatic Approach

1. In order to begin this process, you're going to have to feel absolutely relaxed and comfortable. Using the techniques in the section above can help you to achieve this.
2. Find a focal point in the room that you can watch while you're doing this process. Looking slightly upward and out from yourself is an ideal way to go, like a piece of wall art.
3. Purge your mind of any and all thoughts and simply put all of your focus onto the object in the room that you have chosen.
4. Put your attention (without shifting your gaze) on your own eyes. Think about the movements of your eyelids and feel them becoming heavy as you relax and feel them closing slowly. Put some attention then on your breathing and keep your breathing slow and even.
5. Each time you breathe out, try to focus on relaxing even more than you already were a moment before. This may feel impossible, but you may surprise yourself.
6. In your mind's eye, envision an object moving rhythmically either up and down or side to side. A metronome, a grandfather clock pendulum, a bouncing ball, whatever imagery you choose. Focus on that slow and steady movement with your mind's eye.
7. In your head, count slowly backwards from 10 in a monotone and repeat "I am relaxing" in between each

number. 10. I am relaxing. 9. I am relaxing. 8… and so on.
8. Once you get to the end of your counting, believe that you have reached your hypnotic state and tell yourself that you have achieved that.
9. Your pragmatic prepared statements about your fitness to achieve your goals should be expressed here. **You can achieve what you set out to. Your potential is no longer hidden. Your mind is no longer clouded.** Repeat these statements as many times as you need.
10. Relax once again and allow your mind to clear of all the statements and anything that might have come up along with those. If you experienced any intrusive thoughts, kindly see them out and allow yourself to get back to your most relaxed state.
11. Take your time to slowly count to 10, but as you get higher, increase your energy with each number. In between each number, inform yourself that you will feel completely rested when you "awaken" from your hypnosis.
12. Awaken from your hypnosis and feel completely refreshed! Allow your mind to catch up with you for a couple of moments before you head out into your day or back to your daily activities, then continue on your daily routine feeling revitalized.

A Spiritual Approach

1. In order to begin this process, you're going to have to feel absolutely relaxed and comfortable. Using the techniques in the section above can help you to achieve this.
2. Find a focal point in the room that you can watch while you're doing this process. Looking slightly upward and out from yourself is an ideal way to go, like a piece of wall art.

3. Purge your mind of any and all thoughts and simply put all of your focus onto the object in the room that you have chosen.
4. Put your attention (without shifting your gaze) on your own eyes. Think about the movements of your eyelids and feel them becoming heavy as you relax and feel them closing slowly. Put some attention then on your breathing and keep your breathing slow and even.
5. Each time you breathe out, try to focus on relaxing even more than you already were a moment before. This may feel impossible, but you may surprise yourself.
6. In your mind's eye, envision an object moving rhythmically either up and down or side to side. A metronome, a grandfather clock pendulum, a bouncing ball, whatever imagery you choose. Focus on that slow and steady movement with your mind's eye.
7. In your head, count slowly backwards from 10 in a monotone and repeat "I am relaxing" in between each number. 10. I am relaxing. 9. I am relaxing. 8… and so on.
8. Once you get to the end of your counting, believe that you have reached your hypnotic state and tell yourself that you have achieved that.
9. Inform yourself of the truths that exist in this universe and which you can bring into being. **You are a force of nature. Your motives align with the universe and are just. Your energies are emboldened by the universe and your spirit fortified with all you need to achieve your goals.**
10. Relax once again and allow your mind to clear of all the statements and anything that might have come up along with those. If you experienced any intrusive thoughts, kindly see them out and allow yourself to get back to your most relaxed state.
11. Take your time to slowly count to 10, but as you get higher, increase your energy with each number. In

between each number, inform yourself that you will feel completely rested when you "awaken" from your hypnosis.
12. Awaken from your hypnosis and feel completely refreshed! Allow your mind to catch up with you for a couple of moments before you head out into your day or back to your daily activities, then continue on your daily routine feeling revitalized.

An Emotional Approach

1. In order to begin this process, you're going to have to feel absolutely relaxed and comfortable. Using the techniques in the section above can help you to achieve this.
2. Find a focal point in the room that you can watch while you're doing this process. Looking slightly upward and out from yourself is an ideal way to go, like a piece of wall art.
3. Purge your mind of any and all thoughts and simply put all of your focus onto the object in the room that you have chosen.
4. Put your attention (without shifting your gaze) on your own eyes. Think about the movements of your eyelids and feel them becoming heavy as you relax and feel them closing slowly. Put some attention then on your breathing and keep your breathing slow and even.
5. Each time you breathe out, try to focus on relaxing even more than you already were a moment before. This may feel impossible, but you may surprise yourself.
6. In your mind's eye, envision an object moving rhythmically either up and down or side to side. A metronome, a grandfather clock pendulum, a bouncing ball, whatever imagery you choose. Focus on that slow and steady movement with your mind's eye.

7. In your head, count slowly backwards from 10 in a monotone and repeat "I am relaxing" in between each number. 10. I am relaxing. 9. I am relaxing. 8... and so on.
8. Once you get to the end of your counting, believe that you have reached your hypnotic state and tell yourself that you have achieved that.
9. Your personal statements about your worth, your truth, and your goals should be expressed here. **You are worth it. You are worthy of happiness and success. The pain is in the past and the strength is here today. With the strength within you, greatness is inevitable. All that you want is there for you to take and you can take it today.**
10. Relax once again and allow your mind to clear of all the statements and anything that might have come up along with those. If you experienced any intrusive thoughts, kindly see them out and allow yourself to get back to your most relaxed state.
11. Take your time to slowly count to 10, but as you get higher, increase your energy with each number. In between each number, inform yourself that you will feel completely rested when you "awaken" from your hypnosis.
12. Awaken from your hypnosis and feel completely refreshed! Allow your mind to catch up with you for a couple of moments before you head out into your day or back to your daily activities, then continue on your daily routine feeling revitalized.

A Warrior Approach

1. In order to begin this process, you're going to have to feel absolutely relaxed and comfortable. Using the techniques in the section above can help you to achieve this.

2. Find a focal point in the room that you can watch while you're doing this process. Looking slightly upward and out from yourself is an ideal way to go, like a piece of wall art.
3. Purge your mind of any and all thoughts and simply put all of your focus onto the object in the room that you have chosen.
4. Put your attention (without shifting your gaze) on your own eyes. Think about the movements of your eyelids and feel them becoming heavy as you relax and feel them closing slowly. Put some attention then on your breathing and keep your breathing slow and even.
5. Each time you breathe out, try to focus on relaxing even more than you already were a moment before. This may feel impossible, but you may surprise yourself.
6. In your mind's eye, envision an object moving rhythmically either up and down or side to side. A metronome, a grandfather clock pendulum, a bouncing ball, whatever imagery you choose. Focus on that slow and steady movement with your mind's eye.
7. In your head, count slowly backwards from 10 in a monotone and repeat "I am relaxing" in between each number. 10. I am relaxing. 9. I am relaxing. 8… and so on.
8. Once you get to the end of your counting, believe that you have reached your hypnotic state and tell yourself that you have achieved that.
9. Inform yourself of your warrior statements here. **You are a badass who can achieve anything. What you want is there for the taking and it is ready for you to reach out and take it. Your power has broken its shackles and limits, success is assured.**
10. Relax once again and allow your mind to clear of all the statements and anything that might have come up along with those. If you experienced any intrusive

thoughts, kindly see them out and allow yourself to get back to your most relaxed state.
11. Take your time to slowly count to 10, but as you get higher, increase your energy with each number. In between each number, inform yourself that you will feel completely rested when you "awaken" from your hypnosis.
12. Awaken from your hypnosis and feel completely refreshed! Allow your mind to catch up with you for a couple of moments before you head out into your day or back to your daily activities, then continue on your daily routine feeling revitalized.

Chapter 9: Self-Hypnosis Scripts

This chapter is dedicated to self-hypnosis. If you have an audio downloaded version of this book, this chapter, in particular, should be listened to via audio.

Play the tape and allow yourself to fully immerse in this experience. Find a comfortable place to sit up straight in, or if you prefer, sit on your bed, yoga mat, couch – anywhere that you are alone and undisturbed. Ideally, you will find a quiet place where you feel comfortable enough to fully immerse yourself in the hypnosis. I will give you a prompt when we are beginning a new hypnosis script.

Although some of the descriptions of these scripts have been written with specific themes in mind, it is worth a shot to give all of them a listen to. You will find strength, encouragement, honesty, and motivation in this self-hypnosis. This has been written and designed specifically for your subconscious mind to hear and listen, and for your conscious mind to follow through and take action.

If you do not have this book on audio, you may want to ask a friend or family member whom you trust to read this out for you. In fact, you can invite a friend with similar goals to narrate a self-hypnosis session for each of you! As long as you have given your subconscious mind room to breathe, then this will work. Remember to listen to at least one of these self-hypnosis exercises every day. For this reason, I have written some hypnosis exercises specifically, and some as general goal-strengthening exercises. Take your mind to a quiet place, relax and enjoy.

Self-Hypnosis for Food Addiction and Positive Change

This self-hypnosis is designed for those who have had problems with food addiction in the past, who have struggled with emotional eating, or really, for anyone who has ever felt out of control with their eating habits. In this self-hypnosis, we will be meeting with the version of yourself who you want to become, as well as the version of yourself that you once were, when you were struggling the most with food. The session will now begin.

Welcome to your hypnosis session...
This hypnosis is designed to combat those parts of yourself that are hindering you from living your most authentic self... I invite you to enter this space... that you have set

aside especially... to enter a complete state of calmness... and serenity... This hypnosis is designed to contact your subconscious... which is the true entryway... to all of your feelings... habits... and impulses...

This session uses techniques that are specifically for hypnosis... and guided meditation... to allow you to delve into the greater parts of you... and to tackle food addiction... emotional eating... and anything else that is hindering you from living a happy, controlled, and fulfilling life...

I invite you to sit in a comfortable position... allowing your body to find a relaxing... supported position... You have found a quiet space... and this is your personal time... for self-care, for loving yourself, and for focusing on the goals that are enriching your life... each day at a time...

Now, at this moment... you may want to focus on a particular spot, any spot in the room to focus your vision on... and as you do so... you are feeling your eyes get heavier... and heavier... as this spot in front of you is becoming comfortably blurred... and you are beginning to enter into a state of tranquillity... and peace... As you focus on this spot, you can let your eyes... that are feeling so heavy now... gently start to close... as you succumb to that space within yourself that is the most true... the most you... This place is safe... and you are happy to arrive here...

As your eyes close... you feel your chest gently rise... and fall... as the breaths that come so naturally... and so easy to you... all of the things that make up your body... without you even needing to think about it... are running like clockwork now... and you may now find, as your eyes close... some random thoughts pop into your head... visions... distractions from the outside world... passing by like a drifting cloud in the sky... and you are just observing these thoughts... and allowing them to be... Not connecting any meaning... or feelings towards these thoughts... not judging these thoughts or becoming irritated by them... but just simply letting them be...

And as you drift further... and further... into a state of total relaxation... you find that the thoughts are becoming less... and less... and you feel the euphoric sense of peace... as you enter within you... this is your private realm... and you are meeting with yourself... honestly... and compassionately.

Any noises from the outside world... are drifting in... and out... and they are enhancing this state of trance... and not hindering your descent into a place... of complete awareness... and understanding... and as your chest gently rises and falls... with the rhythm of your breathing... those noises... distractions... thoughts... are feeling further... and further away... and all that is left is this beautiful sense of being... as you are traveling deeper... and deeper... into your innermost self.

Even if your mind drifts... throughout this session... you allow it to... and like a child that has wandered off... you take its hand... and bring it back... into this space of serenity... and without even trying... you are aware that powerful parts of yourself are absorbing this message... that will serve you... your goals... your ambitions... the things that you want the most out of life... as you are enjoying this peaceful feeling of calm...

Everything is as it should be... and you are exactly where you need to be... You have mapped out this time for yourself... solely to be present... to switch off that constant *thinking brain... and to reset those things in your life that are no longer serving your higher self...*

As you are moving deeper... and deeper... into this beautiful sense of calm and relaxation... perhaps the calmest that you have ever felt... you may want to imagine a beautiful, sparkling pool of water... it is a turquoise blue... and it glimmers in the sunlight and welcomes you into its depth... You can now see that there are ten steps... five steps that are out of the pool... and the remaining five, leading into the pool...

And as you gently walk over to this sparkling pool of pure... refreshing... and cleansing water... you stand beside the steps... and you put one foot forward to step down... one... and then two... three... four... five steps... with every step you take, you feel yourself traveling deeper... and deeper... into full concentration... focus... quietness... and at the sixth step... your feet touch the water... and you feel a beautiful sense of relief.. as all of the stress... and held-in tension... and worry... is gradually releasing from your body...

As you feel the beautiful touch of this cleansing... warm water... your legs are beginning to step down further into the water... seven... eight... you feel the touch of the warm water on your thighs... nine... your stomach... and then your chest... ten... as you allow yourself to immerse into this calming, soothing pool of water...

You find yourself floating... peacefully... with the clear blue sky... and the whisper of the breeze... the rustling of the nearby trees... the glowing sun... the delicate chirp of the garden birds... as they sing to you... the Universe is supporting you... and you feel completely safe and secure in this peaceful place... your body no longer needs the support of your limbs and you find that... you are able to float peacefully... and with ease... on top of this clear pool...

In this perfect space... of restoration... and relaxation... you find that my voice... is sounding more and more like your own inner self... and you are connecting to you... the true you... that exists here, in this space... in complete serenity...

You are in a place of total relaxation... this moment is yours... you have chosen this moment especially for you... to give love, hope, and consideration to the things you wish for from the Universe... This is your sacred place... you are moving with the rhythm of the water... and every part of you is supported... by this ebbing... and flowing... of the gentle currents...

With a clear mind, and clear intentions, consider your journey with weight loss so far... I know it has sometimes been difficult, and you have felt alone... isolated... misunderstood... I know the wants and the goals that you desire for yourself... and the Universe desires these for you too... You are ready to set up your life with measurable results... You are getting ready to embark on one of the most important journeys of your lifetime...

As you approach your new life... allow yourself to visualize the person that you are becoming... What do they look like? How do they feel? Imagine a version of you that is free from the restraints of food addiction... This person does not know food addiction... They are confident, happy... they are in control... and this control is within you right now... It has always been within you...

You have the power and the access to control every action... every thought... and as you are falling deeper and deeper into this perfect state of being... you feel at total oneness... from the power that you hold within... The person that you are right now... the person that you have always been... has immeasurable potential... immeasurable opportunity.

You have lost control in the past... you have put on excess weight and you have eaten too much... you may have even committed actions that have directly sabotaged your process... but this is not the space to blame yourself... you need to meet with the old version of yourself here... the one who does not have access to all of the wonders of a healthy life...

Think about a time in your life when you were the most unhappy with your relationship with food... Now, visualize this version of yourself... The broken version... The hurt version... The version that you hide from everyone else... Why is this version of you eating their feelings? What needs to change in order for that to stop happening?

Gradually, right in front of you... you see the older version of you... the you that has struggled with weight loss... who has felt out of control... at a loss... and often alone. This version of you is struggling to float in the water... They are moving their body and becoming frightened... They are afraid that they will drown... but you know that this water is protecting you... and all this older version of yourself needs to do is trust the current... go with the ebb and the flow of the water... and allow themselves to feel the immeasurable support from the water...

Gradually, as the older version of you sees this calm, serene, in control version of you... they start to mirror your actions... and now the older version of you is floating with this new version of you. The you that has been nurtured and supported throughout this journey.

Now let us think about where you are right now, in the present moment... How are you feeling about your relationship with food? ... have your actions in the past 24 hours helped or hindered your journey? ...is there something in the present you that is negatively impacting your weight loss goals? Ask yourself... with sincerity and clarity... "Am I doing enough?" ...are you practicing bad habits or are you forming healthier, new ones?

I want you to meet with this version of yourself and give them the warmest hug. We are comforting. We are meeting ourselves, even our most broken version of ourselves, with pure love and forgiveness. Tell this version of yourself that they are worthy. They are loved. They are enough. Whatever hurt and pain is preventing this version of yourself from becoming the version of yourself in the future, the happier, more content version of you, meet with that pain now.

Give this older version of yourself compassion, care, and love. Tell them that "It does get better!" "You are beautiful." "You are enough." Envision all of that pain and that hurt, breathe it all in and gather it up into your breath... one... two... three... four... and release it with the exhale of your breath... feel the hurt release from your body and dissipate into the water... This is a place of healing... This is a place of recovery... This is who you are meant to be.

You without the burden of past pain, you are with hope... with strength... with endurance...

Every day you are closer to your goals... Every day your goals grow stronger, they get closer. You are exactly where you need to be. Everything is as it should be.

Now, as you slowly bring yourself to consciousness, you will awake with a wonderful sense of newness. Now, you can choose to live as the supported, confident, and in control version of yourself. Everything that you need to succeed is already inside of you.

Gently, and in your own time, slowly open your eyes and bring yourself back to full consciousness. Now, you are awake.

Beautiful Gastric Band Hypnosis

Hello and welcome to this delightful meditation that will guide you along a beautiful beach walk, allowing you deeply relax. Let me be your guide on this mental vacation as we place a mental and emotional gastric back around your stomach, which allows you to feel a delightful fullness as soon as you eat exactly as much food as you need.

Get into a comfortable seated position, preferably your favorite spot, so that you are able to remain undisturbed for the duration of this session. The more you relax, the gastric band becomes even more powerful and influential over your life.

Take a big deep breath in to relax you and exhale tension and worry as you softly close your eyes. Begin to feel your body already slowing down...

Take another breath at your own pace and let to go with a sigh... this moment is for you, so that you practice your new lifestyle, of being full, at the perfect time for you.

Now say to yourself with conviction, "Overeating is impossible for me."

And breathe into the truth of these words. Breathe them out, into reality. Creating a smaller stomach already.

Good...

Relax... breathe... and use the power of your imagination to visualize a beautiful beach with white sand, reflecting in the sunlight... it almost looks like snow... you see the turquoise waters fade to a deep blue as the ocean gets deeper...

Look down into the sand where you stand, noticing beautiful bits of shells all different colors and textures... you see dried seaweed scattered about... something catches your eye half buried in the sand, it is your favorite color, so you get closer. You see it is a small yet thick band, about as big around as your fist... and just so happens that it is the most vivid version of your favorite color. The brightness of this hue brings you joy... this curious, round band, flashing your most beloved color choice is called a gastric band...

It is meant to be placed around the top of your stomach organ, cinching down the amount in which your stomach can hold. In other words, it makes your stomach smaller, giving you the feeling of fullness when you've had enough to eat.

This kind of band exists in the medical word, and the procedure is expensive. However you can get the same results, using the power of your creative mind, by placing this band around your stomach within this relaxing session. But before you do, walk along this beach, Carrying your gastric band... feel it in your hand... notice the texture, the width, and the weight...

Feel your feet in the sand... allowing each step to relax you more and more... notice the powdery texture, dispersing under your feet... let it deeply soothe you.

You can feel the ocean breeze, and smell the salty air... this beach is gorgeous...

As you walk, you get a little tired from how relaxed you are... a perfect chair has appeared just for you, facing the ocean... so have a seat and recline back... you still have your gastric band in your hand, you are familiar with its shape and size now... its like a small belt that can be tightened and loosened.

Relax back in the chair and look out upon the horizon. Notice the ocean melting with the sky.... The clouds are gliding along ever so slowly on a bright blue backdrop. No one's around you... it's peaceful... relaxing... it's gorgeous... Feel the serene sun on your skin, kissing you with nutrients... notice the warm sand under your feet... it is soft and grounding...

Allow your breaths to become a little bit deeper and heavier...listen to the calming sound of the air coming in and out...it is similar to the sound of the waves crashing on the shore...

Take a long deep breath in through your nose, imagining the waves... and a long deep exhale out from your mouth... coming in and out... just like your breath...

Focus intently on the relaxing and calming sound of the waves... gaze out upon the ocean in front of you...

See the crystal-clear waters rippling in the beach wind and reflecting the rays of light... making the surface of the water dance...

If your mind starts wandering and you see some negativity or doubts about weight loss show up...breathe into it... let a wave come and take that thought back out to the ocean as you exhale...

Take a deep breath in....feel that you and the waves are one in the same... exhale a long breath out...feel the sensations of your worry and negativity about your weight flush away... dissolving... becoming less distracting in your mind...

Repeat this beautiful process of letting go of self-doubts...

Deep breath in....into the waves...deep breath out...feel the sound of your negative self-talk begin to wash away... let it all go..

One last time...make the most of it...

Deep breath in….into the waves…let them recollect all your thoughts, your negativity and worries about overeating… and long deep breath out…feel them crashing and disappearing… going away forever…

Feel how you are finally freeing yourself from all that anxiety and stress… you feel brand new….recharged…rejuvenated….lighter….

Self-Hypnosis for Emotional Eating

This self-hypnosis is for those who are likely to respond to food from an emotional perspective. If you feel that you try to self-soothe with overeating, have a greater tendency to binge when feeling down, or if your relationship with food is directly impacting your mental health, then this will be a particularly powerful self-hypnosis for you.

This is about speaking to your subconscious and letting it know, in those times of temptation, that you are in control and have the ability to say no. There is also mention of healing and allowing yourself to reach for other healthier coping mechanisms.

Please note, self-hypnosis is not to be replaced by professional therapy. If you think that some of the issues that come up for you in these sessions are difficult to deal with, you should contact a therapist or health professional to get some support and advice.

Welcome to your self-hypnosis session for emotional eating... I invite you here today... to take this space as a sacred state of being... where you are taking time to nurture the value of being present... You are allowing your body to get into a relaxed state now... as you slowly submit to a complete calm and tranquil space... and your eyes close gently... to immerse yourself deeper into this peaceful place...

All of the tension that you have carried throughout the day... is beginning to ease and melt... with every breath you take... as you enter this self-hypnosis session, and allow yourself to fully commit to the time that you have allocated for this.

Any background noise... the slamming of a door... the closing of the day with the birds chirping... the quiet tapping of an animal's feet... all start to blur into the background as you become immersed inside your innermost authentic self... You may want to picture a tranquil monotonous setting, with blooming flowers and freshly cut grass... and as you take a deeper breath in through your nose... you are taking in that pure air of the mountains... and you feel an overwhelming sense of peace... as you enjoy the beauty and the tranquility of this space that you are allowing your mind to be immersed in.

You know that at any moment, you could come back to full consciousness by simply opening your eyes... and yet, you find yourself present and committed to this moment, this opportunity, to meet with your subconscious mind and let it know all that you desire.

You know that everything that you desire for yourself is within your control and you are comfortable and confident in your ability to reach your goals... As you imagine this monotonous region... you smell the blossoming of the trees and the flowers that grow beside you... and are in harmony with you... You smell the hot air from a warm summer's day... and here you are perfectly at ease... There is nowhere else you need to be but here... in this moment... dipping down into that space with which your truest self exists.

As you enjoy this tranquil space that you have created for your mind to relax... you are inspired by more and more visions, ideas, and inspiration on increasing your health and permanently overcoming emotional eating and every bit of hold that it has on you... more and more to do with increasing your own health and expanding your own vitality... as you are choosing in this time to enhance your very own lifestyle and permanently build greater self-value, self-worth, and well-being.

And so as that deeper part of you continues to envision and structure a healthier lifestyle, one that is free from the restraints of emotional eating... I want you to really believe, every single part of you, that this time is a success story that you are going to enrich other people's lives with... You are honoring your body by maintaining a close relationship with delicious, nutritious whole foods that leave you satiated and complete.

You know that in the past, you attempted to fill a void, that which we call emptiness... and you turned to food to fill this emptiness... This is a normal and common reaction, but you now know that going to food in replacement of looking deeper inside yourself is not serving you... You know that eating in a state of emotion and overeating when you are emotional is a habit that you used to give into.

Now, you have heightened awareness... in this space, where you have practiced discipline, quietness, peacefulness, and meditation, you are strengthening all of those things that prevent you from emotionally eating... Now, in this deep and intimate space that you have built for your mind to relax... and recharge... you know that there is nothing to be afraid of... You are complete... You are whole... You do not go to food to fill a feeling of voidness...

Now, I want you to picture that monotonous region... with the blossoming trees... all fascinating colors that capture your attention... As you happily roam through this unspoiled countryside... and as you turn a corner, there is a small rock pool with beautiful and pure drinking water... and it sparkles with the bluest glint... This pure and mineral-rich water cleanses your body and will leave you feeling inner peace and joy.

As you kneel closer to the rock pool, you scoop some water into your hands and into your mouth, and the refreshing, pure and cold water reaches your lips, and then your mouth, and then flows down through you… and as it flows down through your body, from the roof of the mouth to the tip of your toes, you feel complete.

This stream is cleansing you… healing you… and most importantly, it is replenishing you… This stream comes from a true, deeply connected love for yourself… You are powerful… You are committed to a life of longevity… and you are in control of your emotions…

Every time you think… purely out of muscle memory, to reach for food when you are stressed, sad, angry, or overwhelmed, I want you to visualize this stream… This stream is made from your innermost authentic self… it has been formed by you, in this space, that you have carved out of your day… to become aware… to strengthen your goals… and to remind yourself that you are enough. And when you wake up, you will be brought to complete consciousness, with a new and awakened sense of self. Have a blessed day.

Chapter 10: More Weight Loss Management Techniques

There are so many ways in which you can boost your weight loss progress. Since everyone is different and since methods must change to suit each individual, you should find the methods that speak to you, that sound like a good fit for you, and which you can easily implement into your routine to make very effective change in your weight, in your relationship with food, and in your lifestyle in general. Here are some methods, tips, and techniques for you to consider!

Food Journaling
When you're trying to lose weight, it can be exceedingly helpful to look at the things that you're eating each day. Doing so can give you the perspective you need to understand where the weight gain might be coming from. If you can, start your food journaling before you make any of the necessary or helpful changes to your daily routine. This can give you the full picture of where you started in terms of your daily nutrition and intake. Looking back at how far you've come in just a couple of months will help give you a little bit more pride, wind in your sails, and confidence to keep going! Just remember, if it goes in your mouth, it goes in the journal. Weight loss and health begin with accountability!

Be Mindful
Practicing mindfulness in everyday life can help give you a good perspective on the behaviors you exhibit that you may not even realize. This technique can be so effective with weight loss because so many of us eat without realizing we're doing it, we snack without realizing we aren't all that hungry, and we reach for foods that don't necessarily nourish our bodies in any way. By practicing mindfulness with your eating, meal

planning, and weight loss goals, you are giving yourself the chance to move past those subconscious behaviors and to succeed in spite of the things that your subconscious mind could be doing to trip you up along the way. Mindfulness can be practiced in a few different ways; find the way that speaks to you the most and run with it!

Find Good Outlets
Many of us turn to food when we could be turning to something that is more productive, rewarding, helpful, nourishing, or constructive. If you find that you're home a lot or you're around food a lot and you have a hard time keeping yourself from snacking, munching, or having too many meals throughout the day, you may need a better outlet. Find something that will occupy your time, keep you engaged, keep your hands busy and your attention fixed on something that matters to you so that you can be free of that mental and oral fixation on food throughout the day or even just in your evenings. Evening snacking can be a huge weakness for some, particularly after a stressful day, so make sure you've got relaxing, yet engaging activities planned for yourself.

Get Active
Find something that inspires you to move and run with it. Staying active for a small portion of each day can drastically reduce your risks for heart disease, obesity, and other related illnesses and complications. Try to make it a point to dance, walk, run, stretch, or move throughout your day so you're not staying too sedentary. Especially with the way the world is right now, more and more people are stuck at home with too little physical activity to keep them feeling vital and motivated. Try starting your morning with a walk or taking a break in the afternoon to see the world around your home or office and see how that serves you. Who knows? You might just find an activity you can't live without!

Analyze Your Triggers
If you are an emotional eater, figure out what it is that sets you on that path. Figure out what things cause you to need to eat the most. The more you know about what causes you to veer off your plan of healthy eating, the better you can do at setting yourself up for success and circumventing those triggers. For instance, if you know that a stressful day at work makes you want a very large dinner, snacks, and dessert, then you may want to have some foods at home that are healthy, keep the snacks and desserts away from the house, and make sure that you have something rewarding or enjoyable to look forward to in your evening after that stressful day. And make sure to set these things up in advance. If you wait until that response is triggered, you may find it impossible to fight the urge in that moment!

Drink Plenty of Water
Never underestimate the power of a properly hydrated person. If you have never put importance on proper hydration before, prepare to be amazed. There are so many things that can be cleared up simply by drinking enough water throughout the day. Simply drink 8 ounces of water at a time, 8 times throughout your day. If you need help remembering when to drink, you can set alarms on your phone. If you are worried about spending a lot of time in the bathroom, simply don't exceed that 8 ounces within a 15-minute period so your body has adequate time to absorb and make use of the water you're giving it! In just a couple of weeks, you will find that your head is clearer, your skin is smoother, and your overall well being is vastly improved.

Get Plenty of Protein, Especially in the Mornings
Having enough protein in your day means that your body is getting enough fuel to help it get through everything. Protein is a great source of energy for your body. Many of us have inadvertently shifted to carbohydrates being the main source of fuel. This can make you feel fuller right after the meal, but

it will leave you feeling hungrier later and, depending on the quality of those carbohydrates, could lead to a steep crash in blood sugar later in the day. This can cause food cravings, hunger sooner than usual, or feeling like someone has placed a 1200 lb. boulder on your back so you can't get your cheek up off your desk to keep going with the day after 3 PM. We've all felt the sugar crash after someone brought donuts into the conference room. It's imperative that the calories you eat are meaningful and protein is an excellent way to do that.

Drink Little Bit of Black Coffee in the Mornings
Coffee can sometimes get a little bit of a bad reputation when it comes to its place in a healthful regimen. A little bit of black coffee in the mornings can help you to feel energized and the antioxidants in it can help you feel your best! Eliminating things like cream and sugar can help you to shed extra pounds, especially if you're someone who tends to use a lot of those things each morning. There are plenty of plant-based and sugar-free alternatives that you can use in your coffee if you depend on it to get you going in the morning, but consider dialing back on those gradually so that you get more of the benefits of the coffee and fewer of the drawbacks of the sweeteners. Sometimes, they can cause headaches and they can even trick your body into feeling hungrier sooner! Be vigilant about that sort of thing.

Drink Green Tea
Like coffee, green tea is packed with antioxidants and just a little bit of caffeine to help you to get your day off to a great start. Unlike coffee, however, green tea doesn't have a bold, bitter flavor to it that people tend to like to mute with cream and sugar. You can add things like some mint leaves or just a tiny dash of honey to your tea and you've got a delicate flavor that is as refreshing as it is energizing! If you find that you have a hard time with drinking things throughout the day that add calories to your intake, consider swapping out for tea instead. You can have it hot for a nice comfort in the cooler months

and you can ice it and take it on the go for a refreshing summer beverage as well!

Try Intermittent Fasting
Intermittent fasting is *not* for everyone. There are some people who simply cannot make it work and there is nothing wrong with that. However, if you can comfortably and strategically stagger your meals in such a way that reduces your calorie intake and boosts your metabolism, then intermittent fasting may be for you! Those who swear by intermittent fasting will often fast from dinner time until breakfast, giving their bodies plenty of time to process through any fat that is left behind from a history of overeating, and allowing their bodies to stabilize their metabolic hormones. Take a look at the many fasting schedules that are out there and see if any of those seem like something you could comfortably do and ease into it!

Keep Track of Your Calorie Intake
This one often goes along very closely with keeping a food journal. It's part of keeping yourself accountable for each calorie that you take in throughout the day, and it can even be a pretty eye-opening experience. Some of us go through life blissfully unaware of how small one serving of potato chips really is! We sit down in the evening with a medium-sized bag of chips, crush it, then look at the back of the bag to realize that it was eight whole servings! No one wants to have to do that math after they've already eaten all of those calories without a second thought. By tracking our calories and being purposeful about what we're eating and how much of it, we're giving ourselves a chance to make those better choices. In many cases, you will find that you've closely regimented your intake for the day and at the end of it, you have a few left over for a cup of berries or other delicious (and nutritious) snack!

Reduce Carbohydrate Intake
If you have been looking into weight loss for some time, you may be very familiar with the concept of lowering your carb

intake to reduce the amount of weight retained and gained. Low-carb diets have been all over the diet market since the 80s and even before. Low-carb, high-fat diets have also been heralded as some of the most effective means by which to lose weight and keep it off. You don't have to go all the way to the extreme with it to have success, however. Simply limiting your carb intake to 1-3 servings per day can have a massive impact on your life. You can shave your intake down to some fruit or grains for breakfast, one small single-serve bag of chips with your lunch, and a piece of bread with dinner and you'll still see a massive improvement. One of the biggest things that puts people into trouble with their weight is not realizing how much they're eating. Keeping track and limiting those things is the key!

Use Smaller Plates for Your Meals
At first look, this one might make you roll your eyes. Believe it or not, having a small plate does make your portions of food look larger. It makes your mind think, "Wow look how full that plate is; I'm gonna love this." And it's right. It's gonna love this, and so is your waistline! Tricking the mind is the first step to undoing a lot of our hardest struggles in life. We tend to get in our own ways without realizing it and if we take control and "trick" the mind into thinking that it's getting what it wants from us, we are more apt to have success when implementing changes that would otherwise feel completely cataclysmic. These shifts in portion sizes would leave you feeling sad, starving, and like you're depriving yourself of something. But if your brain is thinking, "This is so much food," then your stomach will have an easier time following suit. This might not be for you, but there's only one way to find out! Give it a try and see how it affects your relationship with portion sizes.

Stock Up on Healthy Snacks
Having healthy snacks to hand is a great way to make sure you won't resort to snacking on salty, fatty, fried, high-calorie foods when you're feeling peckish. Having to get up and prep healthy

snacks can often keep people from snacking on healthy things, leaving them to get hungrier and hungrier until they break and get something they ultimately would rather not eat. If you keep things on hand that you can eat readily, you will often find that your inclination toward the "bad" snacks will lessen and your hunger won't get the best of you. Keep some sliced cucumbers, baby bell peppers, a little bit of low-calorie dressing, maybe some lunch meat and low-fat cheese, and some rice crackers on hand and you should be able to satisfy just about any snack craving that interrupts your day!

Try Meal Planning
Planning out your meals, snacks, and food intake for the entire week is a great way to make sure you're keeping yourself on track. Additionally, it's much easier on your budget because you can make sure you're buying just the right amount of food to keep you satisfied throughout the week, no additional shopping trips, and you won't end up with things that you don't need. From your meal plan, you can make your shopping list that will help you get everything you need and nothing that you don't need. Going shopping and flying by the seat of your pants is a recipe for disaster and we'll explain more in just a couple of moments. When you plan your meals for the week, plan three meals for each day and two snacks. Make sure that you're getting the proper amounts of protein, carbs, healthy fats, and calories each day. Make sure that the snacks you have to hand are filling, full of fiber, and low-carb!

Try Meal Prepping
We have mentioned that having the right kinds of snacks to hand is an excellent way for you to make sure that you're not reaching for the "wrong" kinds of snacks when the cravings kick up. In addition to this, having meals on hand that you can just heat and eat will keep you from looking at a refrigerator full of fresh, delicious ingredients and calling for a pizza instead of doing the work to prepare the meal. We have all had days that leave us feeling like our energy is depleted, like we don't

want to do anything, and like cooking is the last thing on our minds. It happens to the best of us and it will continue to happen. You can beat that state of mind by keeping fully-prepared, delicious, nutritious meals in your kitchen that take very little effort to eat. Meal prep doesn't need to be as complex and artful as some people on social media make it look, so don't worry! Come up with some dishes you like, find recipes that yield 4-8 servings, whip up a batch, then store it to have later! Curries, stews, soups, slow cooker meals, and pressure pot meals are perfect because you just toss them together and voila!

Stick to the Grocery List
This one is *so* important and I am going to dare to say that this is one every single reader of this book should follow. When you go into the grocery store, keep your list right in front of you and live by it. That list is your code of honor when you walk through that store and you must keep to it or you will face turmoil. Have I been dramatic enough yet? Okay, so when you're in the grocery store, there are displays specifically meant to get you to buy things in them. There are sales on all the sweet, salty, fatty, carby delicious foods they have to offer and sometimes it feels like it's just too good to pass up! But remember when you look at your list, that you didn't intend to come home with 2 for 1 double fudge brownies. Are they on your diet plan? Are they part of your goals for a healthier and happier lifestyle? If they were, then you would have put them on the list! Keep that in mind and let your list guide you to the best possible choices for you.

Check the Serving Sizes
As I mentioned earlier, it's so easy for those less healthy foods to make their way into our daily lives without us realizing just how much we're eating. Junk foods or snack foods aren't meant to fill you up, so if you're eating them to get full, you will feel worse and you will end up consuming several servings of it before you get full. One serving of chips (of most kinds)

is 120-180 calories per serving and that is generally by the ounce. The little "lunchbox" size bags of chips are one serving. The ones you get at the gas station typically have 5-10 servings in them! If you crush one of those with a sub at lunch, you're taking in well over 1,000 calories and you probably won't even be full for very long! Check those labels, make sure a serving size is big enough to warrant the calories, and make sure that you're sticking to those servings so you aren't hiding calories, fat, and carbs from yourself!

Eat Spicy Foods
If you are eating something that is very spicy, you will have a two-fold benefit. The first part of it is that you will not want to overeat because it's spicy! Too much spice can make you feel icky and it can also make your stomach hurt. You have to walk a fine line with the spicy stuff. The second part is that capsaicin is actually very good for you! Your circulation and blood pressure benefit from a healthy amount of capsaicin in your diet, so spicy curries (preferably the ones based with coconut milk and not heavy cream) are great for clearing out your sinuses, adding lots of stewed veggies, helping your blood flow, and keeping your waistline trim! Just make sure you don't supplement with lots of bread and cream to tone down that spice, because those extra calories could trip you up! Make your food spicy enough to limit you, but not so spicy that you need a gallon of milk to cool you down!

Start an Aerobics Routine
If you have never done aerobics before, you might feel a little bit silly the first time you try. It's important to remember, however, that no one is judging you for your exercise routine! Aerobics is about getting your body moving, your blood pumping, and using every movement to make you sweat. It's a lot of great cardio and it has a lot of options for low-impact exercise that could be very beneficial to people who are a little bit heavier. One must be careful with one's joints and aerobics is very accommodating for that while also giving you a workout

that is far and away more effective and tiring than it looks! Find some aerobics routines that you like online, or find a class that you enjoy and get going! I recommend, if you are going off of a video, watch an aerobics routine at least once before jumping in so you know how it works and pay attention to the tips the instructor gives to help you participate.

Lift Weights
Lifting weights is a great method for exercise because it works muscles in a targeted fashion while also burning fat. If you are not sure of how you should position yourself when lifting weights, be sure to look up proper form. Look at yourself in a mirror to make sure you're doing it correctly, and start with lighter weights until you nail it. The form when lifting weights is absolutely essential because it will keep you from getting hurt or over-straining yourself, and because it makes sure that you're giving the proper muscles as much of a workout as you intend. Sometimes, having improper form will put the strain on entirely different muscles without you even noticing and it feels like those other muscles aren't even being worked (because they're not)!

Get 20 Minutes of Cardio
Doctors will often recommend 20 minutes of cardio each day. This means getting your heart rate up over 120 BPM for 20 full minutes. This allows your blood to pump, keeps your veins clear, keeps your heart strong, and it helps you to whittle away at the stores of fat in your body. No shame, most people who don't spend their whole lives in a gym have a bit of excess fat. It's just about making sure you're keeping yourself healthy and that you're keeping that excess fat to a minimum with daily activities and a varied, healthy spectrum of foods. Cardio activities can include aerobics, running or jogging, High Intensity Interval Training, swimming, and so much more. Find an activity that gets your heart rate up that you like doing and dive right in!

Reduce Carbs in Each Meal and Replacing with Veg and Fruits

When you're cutting the carbs out of your daily meals, you want to make sure that you're not just leaving a huge gap in your meals. You don't want to leave the table feeling like you haven't eaten enough and you don't want to let yourself just get hungry later, because that will just lead to more snacking, right? It's important that if you cut some of the carbs out of your meals, you take the care to fill in with healthy fruits and vegetables that will nourish your body and leave you feeling full and satisfied when you leave the table. You don't have to sacrifice your satisfaction for your weight loss. Going hungry all the time isn't going to lead to a happier and healthier lifestyle. It's going to make you grouchy, hungry, and it's going to motivate you to run right back to the foods that you wanted to cut out in the first place.

Get Enough Sleep

In a world that is all hustle and bustle all the time, it can be really easy to downplay the importance and effectiveness of a full night's sleep. Try not to let yourself fall into the habit of excusing bad sleeping habits because doing so can affect every area of your life. Getting too little sleep can slow down your metabolism and it can even prevent some digestive hormones from being produced *at all*. This keeps you from being able to properly digest the foods you eat, making it more likely that you will retain the weight from those foods. Additionally, getting too little sleep can kick up your stress hormones, which can further disrupt your digestion. Most doctors recommend anywhere from six to eight hours of sleep per night, but your personal needs may vary. Shoot for seven hours per night and adjust as you get closer to finding the ideal amount of sleep for you. Once you find your ideal number, stick to it like your life depends on it!

Change Your Lifestyle

One of the bigger pitfalls for people who are looking to drastically reduce their weight is thinking that a short-term diet to lose all the excess will be all they need in order to return comfortably to their normal eating habits. Those "normal eating habits" are what led to that weight gain in the first place and thinking about getting back to those habits for the duration of your diet is just setting yourself up for failure. You want to make sure that your attention is fixed squarely on your goals, your personal health, and your well being. In order to do these things, you will need to change up your entire lifestyle. Commit to foods that you like, commit to routines that you enjoy, and make a new lifestyle out of them. If you can shift your thinking into a new mode and you can decide that you're creating a new, ideal normal for yourself and for your health, you will find it so much easier to stick to. This isn't something you're going to be doing for a while, this is your new life!

Take Your Time when Eating

Like many other things about life, our mealtimes are rushed to accommodate the hustle and bustle of the modern age. If you are rushed when you're eating, however, you will find that your food doesn't digest as smoothly or as well, you don't feel quite as full as you might if you took your time, and you might even get a bit of indigestion. If you take your time to eat, putting your fork down in between bites, taking between 8-12 chews of each bite before swallowing, and taking time to read, enjoy someone's company, or talk in between will give your body time to digest your meal in smaller portions and you will feel fuller on far smaller portions.

Avoid Sugary Drinks

This one might *seem* like a no-brainer, but you have to think in the abstract and be very thorough in your determination about sugary drinks. Most people think "soda pop" or fizzy drinks when they hear the phrase "sugary drinks," but the things that get missed are lattes, punch, fruit juice, sweet tea, and flavored or specialty coffee drinks. If you were to look at the nutritional facts of each drink you have throughout the day, you might be surprised to learn that some of them are no better for you than if you had eaten a candy bar instead. Fruit juice, while it's natural and fruity, can have just as much sugar as an ice cream bar. Some coffee drinks have half as many calories as the average-size meal should have. For instance, a medium chai tea latte made with 2% milk is 240 calories. In those 240 calories, you have 42 grams of sugar and 45 grams of carbohydrates. A regular-size Snickers bar contains less sugar AND fewer carbs than a medium (16 fl. oz) chai tea latte made with the standard 2% milk. What kind of new perspective does this information give your morning routine?

Figure Out Your Ideal Level of Variety and Use It
Some people don't need as much variety in their meal plans as others. It's really important that you figure out how much variety matters for you. Some people can eat the exact same meal every single night and be perfectly content to eat their meals and then resume the rest of their day without another thought. Some people can't stand the thought of leftovers and would rather have something new every single meal. If you are somewhere in the middle, you might want to consider making your meals in batches of 4 servings. Having the same meal for 4 nights in a row is more approachable for many people and you could even make two dinners in batches of four so you have 8 nights worth of dinners and you can alternate between them and have a little bit more variety. The things that you choose to put into your meals is entirely up to you and you can use lighter ingredients to make slightly larger portion sizes if you need some help easing into a lighter meal plan. For instance, if you put lots of bell peppers or cucumbers into your salads, you will find them to be more robust in crunch, flavor, and they'll even feel more hearty!

Barley for Breakfast
Barley is an underestimated grain in my humble opinion. It's rich in vitamins, minerals, and several other plant compounds that are great for you. You'll find plenty of fiber, which is ideal for a healthy digestive system, keeps you feeling fuller for longer after breakfast, and allows you to cut down on the morning snacking in the office on things like bagels and donuts! Barley isn't some miracle grain that will make you shed pounds as soon as you eat it, but it is something that will help you get through your mornings and to feel better over a period of continued use. Consider adding barley to your morning meals with a little bit of cinnamon and you might be surprised by how delicious, easy, and filling it is. You can serve it hot like oatmeal, or you can have it chilled and it's a nice, bright way to start the morning. Berries also make a vibrant, low-calorie splash of color and flavor!

Make Sure Your Salads Are Filling Enough
If you're someone who likes to have salads for lunch, consider whether or not they're filling enough. Do you find yourself hankering for a snack within an hour or so of finishing your salad? If you feel hungry or peckish, it might not be a problem with self-control or mind over matter. You might just be lacking enough calories and macronutrients in your afternoon meal! Make sure that you're getting enough protein, that you have a light source of carbohydrates, that there are some healthy fats, and that there is plenty of crunch and roughage in there. I like to use lean meats or boiled eggs for protein on salads and make sure that they're seasoned well enough that I don't need to douse them in dressing to get great flavor. Make sure that you're using diced up veggies as well; the more colorful your salads, the better! A great tip for making a delicious salad is to chop up fresh herbs like cilantro, parsley, or basil and mix them into your salad. That extra, bold, herbaceous flavor can completely transform your salad from "diet food" to a meal you'll actually enjoy!

Keep Frozen Vegetables on Hand
Getting into a whole new mode of living can feel like a whole lot all at once and some evenings, you're not going to have the energy to chop and steam all the freshest veggies for your meals. Keeping some vegetables that you like in your freezer is a great little shortcut for getting a nice, healthy meal without all the fuss. You can also find plenty of fun medleys in your grocer's freezer these days that can add some fun flavor, color, and crunch to your dinner options. Make sure you check on those nutritional facts labels for any sauces that might come in the mix, but they are usually quite light. Experiment a little bit with the options available, find some favorites, and stock up!

Keep a Veggie Platter on Hand
Veggie platters usually come with a little bit of dip and some nicely cut veggies that are easy to grab and munch. Most trays will have celery, carrots, broccoli, and tomatoes, though there are certainly variations that you can find on the market. If there are things that you like and would prefer to have to hand for your snacking needs, consider making your own veggie tray and keeping it in the refrigerator so you can take from it whenever you get the urge to nibble.

There are so many options out there for healthy snacking. You can find a dressing or vegetable dip that suits your needs, your tastes, and your calorie allowance if you look in the right places. Don't limit yourself; find something you really enjoy eating and keep it on hand so you always have it to rely on. Doing so could keep you from that extra helping of potato chips!

Don't Keep Desserts in the House - Go Out for Them
Keeping desserts in the house means that you have access to sweet foods whenever you have the whim. Many of us are overweight because of those whims and because we are unable to fight against those whims when they arise. By leaving desserts outside the house and making them into something that you have to go out of your way to get, you're putting an extra safety net in place. You have to make the decision to have

that extra portion of sweetness in your day, you have to get ready to go out and get it, drive there, and pay for a single serving since you can't keep it at home. All of these things, though they might seem simple at first glance, are all additional opportunities for you to either rethink the decision, or to keep you from making that decision as frequently as you might otherwise do!

Friday Skinny Clothes Routine
Each Friday, take a little bit of time to do a private fitting with your "skinny clothes." If you have a goal outfit to fit into, it gives you something tangible to look forward to. Your goals feel that much closer when you can envision them and when you can see how close or far you are to them. Having that routine helps you to keep your attention centered on the goal, and it helps you to visualize the ideal scenario with regularity. Energy flows where your attention goes, so you want to make sure that you have your "eyes on the prize" as often as you can. Doing this will help your goals to come to life much more quickly than they might otherwise! Seeing how close or far you are to or from your goal can also help you to push yourself and stay motivated in your daily routines and in your new lifestyle. Staying motivated is one of the biggest helpers with weight loss!

If You Can Move It, You Can Exercise It
Some people think that exercise has to mean that you're exhausting yourself and working out so much that you can't move the next day. In fact, when you work out so hard that you can't move comfortably or get through the next day, you're setting yourself up for a loss. A good workout is one that gets your heartbeat up, that works out the muscles in such a way that they will improve over time, and which leaves you feeling tired, but not exhausted. You want to feel a little bit of that localized soreness in your muscles the following day, but you don't want it to be so much that you feel discouraged from going back again and doing it again when the time comes. Take

your workouts seriously and think about the parts of your body that you can move. Those parts of your body are controlled with muscles, which could all stand to be stronger. Making stronger muscles often means that the area around those muscles becomes leaner. Start small if you're not used to exercise and work your way up! You can start with a stationary bike and some light weight lifting (make sure to look up proper form and adhere to it!) if you're most comfortable with that, then you can build from there.

Gratitude Journaling
You will often be completely shocked at how much about your life changes when you take the time to be grateful each day! Staying positive and grateful with your gratitude journal can help you to get more restful sleep, which can improve your energy levels and your ability to lose those pounds. Your mental state improving and your energy improving can cause a domino effect that largely benefits sweeping areas of your life in a way that might surprise you. Give it a try. Take up gratitude journaling for a week and see how things change in terms of your mentality, and make a note of your weight loss progress in that time as well. This could just be the key you were looking for!

Don't Skip Meals Willy Nilly
Skipping meals without a planned schedule and without making sure you're getting the proper nutrients can mess up your body's ability to metabolize your food properly. Skipping a meal here and there keeps your body from being able to produce the right hormones in anticipation of your meals, making it harder and less efficient for you to digest the foods that you're eating. In addition to this, skipping meals can make you much more hungry when you do get around to eating, causing you to reach for more food than you need and for foods that provide far less nutritional benefit. When you're feeling like you're starving, you want something hearty and rib-sticking like a chicken parm or like a big sub instead of a leafy

salad or a healthy cutlet of chicken, right? So make sure that if you're skipping meals, you're doing so according to a plan (i.e. intermittent fasting) and that you're keeping all your meals healthy and appropriately sized and portioned.

Amp Up the Flavor
A rookie mistake when beginning to eat healthy is phasing out everything that has flavor in favor of things like lettuce, cucumbers, and celery sticks. These, as I am sure you are aware, have very little flavor on their own and leave you wishing for something like creamy salad dressing or peanut butter to dip them in and I have to tell you, that is a sure fire way to amp up the calories without enough satisfaction to back them up! You need to make sure that you're getting foods with a lot of flavor and that you're seasoning your foods thoroughly when you compose a meal. Find low-calorie sauces and condiments (mustard and hot sauce are two excellent examples) that you can use in your meals, you need to find produce that has robust flavor on its own. Arugula, for instance, is a bitter green with just a hint of spice to it. Instead of regular cucumbers, get English or Persian cucumbers. They are more crisp, have fewer seeds, and their flavor is much more prominent. Use plenty of herbs as well! You should be buying a bundle of fresh parsley, cilantro, basil, mint, etc. each week to use in your salads, dishes, drinks, etc. so your palate isn't ever bored. Being sick of the lack of flavor is the quickest way to chase you off of a diet and into the arms of Ronald McDonald.

Look at the Menu Before Going Out
So much of life is conducted around the dinner table. When someone makes the honor roll, we go out to dinner to celebrate. When someone is having a birthday or an anniversary, we go out to dinner. Until your eating habits become a little bit more restricted, you may not even notice how many things you will miss and how many times per month your family goes out or orders in. It is a horrible feeling to go out to a restaurant, smell those delicious fried foods, and then

have to decide to have a chicken caesar salad for dinner. Something that can really help you with this is knowing what you're going to get when you walk in so your determination is never swayed is making a decision on what you're going to order before you arrive. Take a look at the menu online (most restaurants will have their menus on their websites, even the niche ones) and determine which dishes best suit your needs, your tastes, and your calorie allowances. Now, not all dishes will have the calorie amounts on them so you may have to do some judging of your own to determine how appropriate the dishes are for your needs.

Get a Box with Your Meal
Figuring out what you want before you get to the restaurant is a great step, but there is more to dieting when you go out to dinner that you need to know. In the United States, each meal that you can order in a typical restaurant will have 2 to 3 times the amount of food that you should be eating in a sitting. When you place your order for your food, ask for a box to come with the meal and box up half or more of your food before you even take a bite. Or! Ask the kitchen to bring you half a portion and box the other half. This will give you a very set stopping point in your meal at the restaurant, will keep you from eating too much, and will leave you with leftovers of your delicious meal for the next day!

Stop Eating When You're 80% Full
Some of us who are trying to lose weight have a little bit of difficulty gauging when we truly feel full. Many of us will eat until our stomachs feel so full that we need to unbutton our pants, lie down, or take a breather. It will take some time for you to figure out the appropriate level of fullness. Try to figure out the serving sizes for the foods you are eating and stick to them as a preliminary guideline. From there, you can adjust and find out what "full" means to you. Once you do, eat until you're 80% there. This will allow your stomach to acclimate to

a smaller portion of food over time and will allow you to reduce your waistline as you do so!

If You Can't Eat it, Don't Buy It
Buying foods that don't belong on your diet plan is a great way to set yourself up for failure. Now, if you're not living with other people and you are only shopping for your personal needs, buying things that you cannot eat is very similar to making a promise to break all your new good habits. You're saying "I want to keep this in the house because I am eventually going to want to eat something I shouldn't be eating."

Many of us have to maintain a healthy diet and weight loss with other people in the house who are not on the same regimen that we are. In many cases, this can lead to us needing to buy foods that we cannot eat so the people around us can continue to live their lives as normal, eating the way they always do. In such cases, it might be helpful to you to tell those people that you would no longer like to be in charge of buying those foods. Severing the connection between yourself and those items is a big step toward a healthy lifestyle that is free of those things. Consider also relegating those items to a certain cupboard or cabinet in your home that you never go into so they're not in your line of sight in your regular travels through the kitchen.

Find a Salty Snack and Skip the Chips
For some, salty snacks are kryptonite. Finding the right kind of salty snack to satisfy your cravings without packing on the calories can be a total lifesaver for someone who is trying to live a healthier lifestyle. Thinks like seaweed snacks, nuts, veggie chips, and beef jerky can add plenty of flavor to your day without going overboard on the calories, fat, and carbs. Make sure you look at the labels, though! Some snacks like to parade around like they're some gift to the dieting community, when really they're pants-stretchers in disguise! Look for sodium, fats, carbohydrates, and sugars on those nutritional facts labels, look for strange items on the ingredients lists, and make sure you're not falling prey to creative packaging!

Eat Breakfast
Having something in your stomach in the morning is a great way to start your day. For starters, getting through your morning routine is hard enough without adding those hunger tantrums on top of things! Making sure that you get the right amount of nutrients in your morning can help you to get through your day with much more ease and can keep you from feeling like you need to go all out with your lunch plans. If you are someone who doesn't typically like or eat breakfast, you can gradually get yourself there over time. Simply start your day with something small and unobtrusive like a protein shake or a smoothie and work your way up to full meals if you feel so inclined. Doing so could give you a stronger start to your day and could leave you feeling fuller by the time lunch rolls around.

Take Pride in Your Kitchen
When you're trying to change everything about your eating habits, you're going to be spending much more time in the kitchen than you have in the past. Make it a point to put things in your kitchen that you like using and maybe even put up some artwork to make you feel like you're really at home there. The more you like that space, the more you will enjoy the time that you have to spend there putting your meals together. Consider putting up a stand for your tablet or maybe even a television to help occupy your mind while you're in there. Listening to music or audiobooks is another great way to turn your kitchen into a haven for you while you're preparing your meals for yourself.

Take Pride in Your Cooking
By taking pride in your cooking and by going the extra mile to make sure what you make is beautiful and delicious, you are telling yourself that you are worth that effort. You are telling yourself that you are special company who deserves to be served on the good china. When we take those extra steps to care for ourselves and to prove with our actions that we think

we are worth it, we are more likely to see a hefty return on that investment. When you can take pride in the things that you have put together in your kitchen and the flavors that you create, you will enjoy the "diet foods" that you are supposed to be eating. Just slapping together a depressing, flavorless salad with some dry, baked chicken and calling it a meal will put you on the fast track back to old habits. Take pride in every meal you put together and watch as your friends, family, and co-workers look on with envy that your meals are so much more artfully and deliciously crafted than their "non-diet" options.

Make it Easy to Grab Breakfast on the Go
Our society has seemed to go out of its way to turn the grab-and-go breakfast into a caloric and nutritional catastrophe. Many of the things that we think of when we envision a breakfast on the go are composed of salt, fat, pork, tons of bread, and tons of sugar. This, of course, is not what we mean when we suggest an easy breakfast on the go. What we do mean is taking a little bit of extra time at the beginning of your week to whip up a batch of healthy breakfast options that will keep well, composing a breakfast with them, and setting them up so your morning routine is shortened by using them! Some like to bake a bunch of scrambled eggs and turkey bacon, put it on an English muffin with some cheese, wrap it up, and make heat and eat breakfast sandwiches. Some make little mini frittatas in their muffin tins with all kinds of delicious veggies and meats. Some like to make power protein bars and wrap them up. You could even do a mix of all three if you felt so inclined! If breakfast is easy to grab, you are far more likely to eat it instead of a donut of muffin you might swipe on your way to the office.

Always Have a Backup Meal Plan
Sometimes, you will find that even the best laid plans aren't immune to going up in smoke right in front of your eyes. It is not unheard of for a planned meal to be going off without a

hitch and then suddenly, the whole thing is ruined. Maybe the oven was set too high and the dish burned. Maybe you forgot one key ingredient and the whole thing fell to mush. Maybe your mother called and you suddenly ran out of all the time you needed to prepare your dish. In any such case, the easy answer is always takeout or delivery options, which are bound to increase your calories, carbs, and fat for the day by leaps and bounds! Having a backup plan on deck is the best way to make sure that you won't go running into the arms of the delivery man! Maybe you could have the chopped ingredients for a delicious salad ready to compile. Maybe you could have some leftovers on hand to heat and eat. Maybe you could put together something that requires only a little bit of extra cooking to make something that will wow you. An ounce of prevention is worth a pound of cure, so get creative and keep something delicious on deck!

Don't Eat After Sundown
Now, I know that you're not some mystical creature that will produce other, horrible creatures if fed past a certain time of the night. However, I also know that if you're eating after sundown, you will likely be going to bed within just a couple of hours of eating. Doing so will stop your body from fully and properly metabolizing those foods and will leave you with some extra pounds in the long run. Think of food as fuel for your body. I know this sounds like a cliche, but it is true and thinking of it in such terms will likely be a great help to you. So if food is fuel, that means that you need it in order to run around doing your errands, you need it to do that project at work, you need it to take the dog for a walk, and you need it to get you through that awkward visit with the in-laws. What you don't need fuel for is sleep. When you're sleeping, your body is whittling all its processes down and allowing your body to get a nice, recuperative rest. There is no need to fuel your body before this portion of the day. We say not to eat after sundown, but thanks to the seasons and the changing times of sundown, what we really mean is that you shouldn't be eating past about

7 PM. If you're going to be going to bed within 2-3 hours, it's not necessary to fuel your body with anything that you might be craving in the night.

When Choosing Carbs, Go for the Natural Stuff
Looking at nutritional labels and thinking of carbs only in terms of their quantity can leave us feeling a little bit sluggish from time to time. For instance, some chips might have the same number of carbs as an apple, but the apple will often make you feel more nourished and keep you going for longer than the chips will. Natural carbs tend to stick with you for longer and they tend to bring lots of other nutrients with them that will help you to feel your best as well. Take a look at some of the options you have in your kitchen that contain carbs and ask yourself if those carbs are natural or processed. Then look at ways to increase the number of natural carbs in your kitchen!

Don't Eat Out of the Bag - You Are Not a Horse
Portion control is hard enough when we don't have the whole bag of delicious chips nestled comfortably in our laps. Bringing the bag of snacks to the couch is a terrible idea that will inevitably lead to your eating far more than a serving at one time. When you want a snack, it's best to grab a small bowl or plate, take a serving out of the bag, and serve yourself that way. By using this method, you're putting another set of steps in between yourself and those extra servings. Sure, if you have a calorie allowance for it and you're feeling a little bit snackier than usually, you can go back and grab another serving and it's not a big deal. But at least, with this method, you're snacking consciously and mindfully, which is a huge step in the right direction. It's all these small things that culminate in real weight loss success over time!

Keep an Eye on the Fats You Cook With
It's easy, when you're cooking, to forget that the oils and fats we use to grease our cookware does still contain calories that ultimately end up in our food. If you put a tablespoon of butter

into the pan to cook, a good portion of that butter is going to end up in your food. A tablespoon of olive oil does have calories. Even though the oil is better for you and your body, you will want to take those oils into consideration when you're planning your meals and when you're figuring out how many calories and fats you're putting into your day. Plan on using higher quality fats. Oils from things like olives and avocados are going to be better for you than things like lard, butter, or bacon fat.

Keep Your Water Interesting
Drinking enough water throughout the day can be a real challenge if you find water to be underwhelming or hard to drink in large quantities. If you are someone who likes to drink lots of soda, juice, or other drinks instead of water, it could take some time for you to adjust to drinking nothing but water. Try to find things you can add to your water that will make it more interesting for you. There are flavor syrups with electrolytes that add flavor to your water without adding a bunch of things you don't need. There are powders that will turn your water into a sports drink, and there are tons of fruits and vegetables that you can add to your water to flavor it and keep it tasting delicious. Mint, cucumber, lemon, lime, and strawberries, to name a few! Just like with your dishes, make every bottle of water taste the best it can taste and drink up!

Have Coffee at Home
As mentioned in a previous section in this chapter, there are a lot of drinks in coffee houses that can stack on fat, sugar, carbs, and calories before you even know it. Having your coffee at home means that you're sure of exactly what's going into your cup. Over time, cutting down on those cafe coffees will pay off in a big way. As an additional bonus, when you start drinking coffee at home, you will save a ton of money!

Add Filling Fiber to Your Meals
Fiber is a great way to fill out your meals and to make them feel like they're much more hearty. Often, when you're eating diet-friendly foods, you'll feel unsatisfied and like there wasn't quite enough to what you ate. Filling in with lots of fiber can give you more to munch on, it can help you regulate your digestion, and it will have you feeling fuller for longer. The higher in fiber your vegetables are, the more rib-sticking those meals will be! Look for dark leafy greens that are rich in plenty of vitamins and minerals, look for colorful veggies that have lots of fiber in them, and be very generous about scattering them all throughout your meal plans!

Make Your Salads Crunchy
Having a bit of crunch in your day really helps with those snack cravings. We don't tend to realize how much we rely on things like chips, crackers, and other crunchy snacks to get us through our days until we can't have them. Once they're "not allowed," it seems like they're all that used to tie every meal together. By adding some crunch to your salads with some light croutons, crispy chickpeas, cheese crisps, or nuts, you will feel like your salads are not only more filling, but that the craving for those other salty snacks doesn't come up as much or as often.

Monitor and Reduce Your Stress
Stress has such a profound effect on your body, your well-being, your health, your appetite, and the processes that your body goes through every single day. Stress cannot be underestimated in its ability to affect, change, and damage your life and your health. Make sure that your stress levels aren't going too high and make sure that you're giving yourself plenty of time and ability to let go of and move past stress. If you're stressed, things will always seem harder, especially dieting. If you're trying to lose weight while you're stressed, you're going to notice that things aren't moving at the pace you would like. This will, in turn, lead to more stress that compounds and makes the issue worse! It's imperative that you narrow down

the areas of your life that are causing you stress and that you figure out how to work through that stress. Some people like to journal, some people like to meditate or use aromatherapy, and some people like to take up sports that help them physically work through that stress. Find out what your stresses are, find out the best way to cut back on it, and deal with the remainder in a healthy way.

Replace Your Noodles
Noodles are present in nearly every culture around the world. A delicious noodle with a healthy helping of sauce and some veggies is a classic meal that has about 1,001 variations. Going on a diet means we often have to cut out those dishes that we love, making us feel like we've made the ultimate sacrifice. However, you can still have those dishes if you simply replace the noodles. You can spiralize zucchini and use them as "zoodles," you can use yam noodles that come packaged in water and which taste virtually like nothing, you can use spaghetti squash, or you can find another substitute that works great for you and your needs. Once you replace those noodles, you will find the calorie counts of your dinners dropping dramatically and you won't have to worry about missing out on spaghetti night!

Shoot for 10,000 Steps a Day
Pedometers and fitness trackers are much more widely available and popular today than they have ever been. So much so that they are even built into most smartphones now. Just by keeping your phone in your pocket, you can track how many steps you've taken in a day and you can shoot for higher and higher numbers each day to make sure that you're getting all the daily activity your body needs in order to thrive. Many people use 10,000 steps as a great mark for weight loss. This allows them to get around throughout the day, get a decent-sized walk in each day, and to experience a bit of weight loss as well. 10,000 steps per day is a lot and, depending on your height, could mean walking up to 5 miles each day! You don't

have to start with that if you're only used to walking a couple thousand steps each day. You can work up to it! By making 10,000 steps a daily goal, you're putting your attention on walking more and you will find that over time, your time spent walking will grow and eventually you will be able to get 10,000 steps in before the end of your day without an issue!

Grocery Shop Only when Full
This one is a very popular piece of advice that I'm sure you've heard before. If you go to the grocery store with a grumble in your stomach, you're going to reach for just about everything you see that sounds good to you at that moment. Sure, you can go in with a list and stick to it, but you might find that you were distracted by that colorful display of snack cakes, or the bags of chips that were so conveniently placed right by your checkout aisle. It's a slippery slope to go into a grocery store that is full of temptations when you're trying to have a better, healthier relationship with yourself and with your food. Consider having a light snack before you go shopping so that no matter what comes up, you can stick to the list, get everything on it, and come home with nothing except the groceries you needed and a sense of accomplishment.

Don't Underfeed Yourself
A common mistake in dieting is removing too many calories from one's menu during the week. It's possible to undereat during the day and leave yourself feeling faint, hungry, and wobbly. For some, having too few calories can lead to headaches, fatigue, and lack of strength. An average daily diet is typically made up of 2,000 calories. By reducing this number slightly and by increasing the quality of the calories being consumed, it is possible to lose a good deal of weight in a short time. It's not always easy to trim yourself back to about 1,800 or 1,600 calories per day, but you will find that the more you focus on it and the more you try, the easier it will become to adjust to that amount and your body will eventually thrive on it! Many people have found that after just the first few weeks,

this regimen becomes a matter of habit and it feels almost as though they don't have to force themselves to stay away from the foods that would push them over their calorie limits.

Moderation is Key
Often when the subject of dieting is broached, people want to talk about what foods are being cut from your diet. It may come as a surprise to you to learn that you don't actually *have* to cut anything out of your diet at all in order to lose weight, unless the foods in question are causing an allergic or negative reaction that would cause you to retain weight. Let's take an extreme example here and talk about it. Say you have a strong liking for sweet pastries. You particularly like those little pies that are filled with fruit. Now, it's a cruel blow to realize that each one of those pastries can be as many as 450 calories each with an astronomical amount of sugar. *However*, that doesn't mean you can't have any! You can simply cut the pie into quarters and allow yourself to have a piece each day or every other day. So long as the rest of your foods are healthy, you're getting plenty of physical activity, and you're sticking to smaller servings, you can have almost any food *in moderation*.

Allow Yourself to Savor Your Food
In this section, we have covered taking your time to eat your meals. Doing so will allow you to feel more full by the time you're through and it will allow you to enjoy the food that you're eating. We've also covered taking pride in the things that you create in your kitchen. Marry those two and we have this piece of advice: savor your food. Really take the time to see the flavors in your dish, make each bite count, and give yourself at least 20 minutes to finish the meal. You can put your fork down between bites, take a little extra time to chew your food than normal, and you can let the flavors sit for a couple of moments before taking your next bite. It might seem like a simple and silly thing to insist upon, but you will be amazed about how much this one aspect will affect your ability to enjoy and feel satisfied by your food.

Eat Out Less
Going out to restaurants or ordering in is something that adds plenty of calories to your diet before you can even blink. The salads are loaded down with fatty dressings, the meals come out at two to three times the servings sizes we ought to be having, the foods are sometimes packaged before they get to the restaurants with oil and preservatives, the foods are cooked in oil or deep fried, and the calories just abound. And that's without an appetizer or a dessert! Eating out can mean that you are taking on far more calories than you ever realized and it can also be a huge drain on your wallet. In addition to this, if you're not cooking at home, you're missing out on a lot of opportunities to take pride in what you're cooking and eating, and you will often miss out on opportunities to savor your food, as busy restaurants are often trying to empty their tables just as quickly as they filled them so they don't have a ton of hungry diners waiting for tables. Consider how many times you eat or order out during the week and consider how many calories are in the dishes that you get. See where you could make some cutbacks to improve your experience!

Keep a Balance
When trying to bring down your weight, it's imperative to remember that you're trying to achieve and restore balance to your body. You don't want to be overweight, but you also don't want to be *underweight*. You want to make sure that you're getting all the right foods and just enough of the "bad" ones to make things interesting. Keeping a balance in your life is the best way to achieve lifestyle change. Being too drastic in one direction or another isn't quite sustainable and it can leave you feeling like you're wanting for something or like you're just cheating yourself. Achieve balance in your meal plans, in your lifestyle, and in your nutrition. That is how you will feel your best and achieve the most success.

Don't Demonize Foods

You may have noticed that in this section, when I've referred to "bad" foods, I've put them in quotation marks. The reason for this is that it doesn't help to think of the more indulgent foods as bad. This simply introduces a self-denial complex and a demonization of something that you have ultimately enjoyed over time. Now, if you're someone who has found processed foods to be unenjoyable, then congratulations! You don't have to eat them and severing ties with those foods in order to obtain your goals and successes will be all the easier. Demonizing foods that we once enjoyed can lead us to beating ourselves up for ever liking them in the first place. Those fatty, salty, greasy, or sweet, creamy, sugary foods are specifically created to be enjoyed. Enjoying these foods doesn't mean there is something wrong with you. Rather than swearing off these foods altogether and branding them with a "bad" label will only make you feel more guilty if you do end up having some every once in a while. Instead, think of them as "moderation foods." These are foods that, if they made up your whole diet, would have severely negative repercussions. You'd be sluggish, gaining weight, your skin would break out more often, and you might just feel terrible if you lived solely on processed snack foods! However, if you have a balanced diet with plenty of fruits, vegetables, lean proteins, fiber, vitamins, and minerals, having one of these snacks every so often isn't going to have any negative, lasting effects. Think of them as moderation foods and you won't feel the need to deny yourself of them anymore. You just have to place them strategically throughout your meal plan!

Use Gum to Curb Cravings

Being used to eating regularly throughout the day can make it hard to regulate your intake. Your mouth is constantly occupied with chewing those foods and you might even start to feel a little bit of anxiousness for lack of that occupation. Using gum can give you the feeling that you're eating without giving you those extra calories. Gum also comes in plenty of unique flavors to keep your palate interested and occupied. Mint is also a palate cleanser, which means that it will be harder for you to dream up those memories of flavors, which can trigger cravings! Stock up on some of your favorite sugar-free gum and chomp on a stick whenever you feel like you might start getting some cravings! If you're like me and you're not big on some of those artificial sweeteners that are on the market, consider looking into gums that are sweetened with xylitol and erythritol. They're natural, calorie-free sweeteners that don't have a strange aftertaste!

Avoid Frying Your Food
This one might seem like common sense, but there are more methods for frying than just the deep vat of boiling fat. Putting your foods into pans with lots of melted butter, several tablespoons of hot oil, or using oil to get that unique crunchy crisp on your foods all count as frying! You can even fry an egg with the right amount of oils in a pan. Doing each of these things, even with the healthiest of ingredients, can significantly reduce the health benefits of your meals. It can also drastically increase the fat, salt, and calories in your meals. Avoiding this type of cooking will, in the long run, do you a lot of favors.
Consider baking your meals or trying air-frying them if you're still looking for that crisp! Doing so will give you a lot of flavor, but significantly cuts down on the amount of fat you are required to add to your meals.

Foist Fattening Leftovers Off on Guests
When you have friends or family members over for a large meal, it's natural to want to go all out with the dishes! Maybe make a pie, some creamy sides, and some delicious bread to go along with it all. There is nothing wrong with making an indulgent meal like this every so often. However, if you're left with enough leftovers to eat for about a week, then you're getting those same calories, fat, carbs, etc., several days out of the week. Try giving your guests plates to take home with them so you're left with very little. Doing so always makes your

guests feel like they've gone out to a fancy place, and it saves you from a whole week of meals you wouldn't usually plan for yourself when watching your weight!

Measure Portions Before Getting to the Table
You may have heard of serving dishes Family Style. This means bringing large platters and dishes of food to the table so everyone can serve themselves and go back for seconds very easily. This is something to avoid so you know exactly how much you're portioning out for yourself for each meal. Additionally, it puts extra steps between you and that extra helping. Sure, you can go back for another plate if you feel hungry enough, but it should be a conscious decision to do so if you're trying to eat mindfully and to be fully aware of what calories you're taking on throughout the week.

Ask for Dressing On the Side
A serving of salad dressing is typically 1-2 tablespoons. Often when a salad is served to you in a restaurant, it is given to you with a small ladle of dressing that isn't exactly measured out each time. Asking for your salad dressing on the side allows you to add a little bit of dressing to your salad at a time so you can get all you need without going overboard on the calories that salad dressings often contain.
Going with a lighter salad dressing option is an optimal choice, but if you're getting a smaller amount of even the lower-calorie options, you're really making the most out of each meal that you have!

Be a Picky Eater
People who aren't picky about what they eat will often consume things that don't necessarily provide any benefit for them. The crusts on sandwiches, the extra bits of tortilla on an overly-wrapped burrito or salad wrap, and tons of other things that we don't even tend to think about. Start looking at all the things you eat and ask yourself if you really, truly enjoy every single bite. If you don't, cut out the bites that you don't love!

Doing so will cut back the calories here and there and doing that all throughout your day, every day, will add up to a lot of calories trimmed out of your diet without you even noticing it!

Take 20 Minutes to Distract from Cravings
When you notice that you're starting to crave foods that you would rather not be eating, take 20 minutes to distract yourself with things that interest you or that keep you engaged. Consider doing some chores around the house, doing some light reading, coloring or working on a craft that you enjoy, playing some games, or doing some other activity that you enjoy that occupies your mind. Generally, it's best to avoid television when you're craving food, particularly if you are someone who has spent a lot of time snacking in front of the TV. It's all about spotting those patterns in your behavior and interrupting them for the better!

Rinse Your Mouth with Mouthwash to Neutralize Cravings
In this section when we talked about using gum to interrupt cravings, we talked about how the flavorings in gum can cleanse the palate so those cravings can't quite take hold like they otherwise would. This is the same principle in play with this piece of advice. Brush your teeth or use mouthwash to cleanse the palate and also to activate that part of yourself that says, "I just cleaned my mouth, it would be a waste to eat right now and get it messy again," or even simply "nothing would taste very good right now." It might seem silly, but you could give it a couple of tries and see if it does anything to help you with that impulse!

Track Your Progress
Watching your progress with weight loss can be a great motivator. If you're looking for that progress, monitoring it, and working toward changing that number with each passing week, you just might find that your weight loss follows that attention and that you feel more reward over time. In addition

to being able to see how you're doing, you will find that tracking your progress will keep your "eyes on the prize," so to speak. If you're always thinking of your weight loss progress and you're always thinking about ways to maximize on that, then you're going to find it easier to keep to what you should be doing without all the distractions of everyday life coming in when they shouldn't be.

Reward Yourself
Give yourself some incentives from time to time if you think that will help motivate you toward the goals that you've set. Make sure that your rewards don't involve food, but also make sure they're things that you really want. You'll buy yourself that game you've been wanting to play, take yourself out for a nice date to the local museums, go see that movie you've been looking forward to, or give your wardrobe a little update. Pick something that means something to you and use it to lure yourself closer and closer to your goals!

Chapter 11: Facts & Myths about Self-Hypnosis

Myths

Under hypnosis, you can only tell the truth and you can even tell your deepest secrets

It is a classic caricature of hypnosis that the person is put into a fugue state with some deep connection to their subconscious. Their mouth, in these caricatures, seems like a tap into that subconscious that can be used at will by the hypnotist. This is not the case. Someone who is hypnotized still has control of themselves, their mind, and their speech. They simply have the ability to place more suggestions and affirmations into their minds without difficulty and, in some cases, are able to spot the things that don't belong there and pull them out. Being able to do such a thing allows one to get rid of the hidden suggestions and conclusions that have been holding them back for years without them noticing.

You will have no memory of the hypnotism itself

Think of every depiction of hypnosis you've ever seen wherein the person under hypnosis did something embarrassing or silly. In those cases, did the person ever seem to remember what it was they had been doing under the suggestion of the hypnotist? Typically such depictions show the person sheepishly wandering back to his seat with nary a clue as to what has gone on while all his friends smile knowingly at one another about what has just transpired. Thankfully, this is not something that is typical, usual, or acceptable in hypnotherapy. It's important also to note that there is a difference between stage hypnosis and hypnotherapy.

People cannot be hypnotized are always of high intellect
Many people have written journals, musings, articles, and opinion pieces about an intelligence quotient threshold for those who are able to be hypnotized. In many such cases, the writers theorize that people with IQs barely sufficient to operate a vehicle or write one's own name are the only ones who can be effectively hypnotized. This is incredibly reductive, offensive, and entirely untrue. Intelligence has very little to do with one's ability to submit to that deep level of relaxation and to a place of receptiveness to the subject of subconscious suggestions. Some people simply can't get into that mode and it's nothing to do with their intelligence or anything else they can or should want to control; it simply isn't for everyone, just like every other therapy that exists.

Someone who is hypnotized can get stuck that way
Think back to when you were a child and your mother told you that if you continued to cross your eyes or make an ugly face, you would get stuck that way, unable to bring it back to its normal state. Think back on that statement now and realize how silly that sounds to you. This is also the case for hypnotism and you cannot get stuck in that state any more than you can fall asleep and stay that way or stay drunk forever. These states of mine and subconsciousness are temporary *always* and what you do with your thinking in the time you spend in these states is entirely up to you, and will not affect their duration.

Being hypnotized is similar to being asleep or unconscious
Being asleep is the only thing the human body can do that is like sleep. Being unconscious is even distinct from sleep in medical terms. Hypnotism requires that you be awake so that you can answer questions, so you can make observations, and so you can benefit from the therapy. There seems to be a line of thinking with certain things in life that one can simply be put to sleep by some unusual or atypical means, have some

simple procedure done to or for them, and wake up cured or better than when they went in. It is of dire importance that you realize and come to terms with the fact that absolutely nothing in your life will change for the better unless you are awake, giving attention to it, and actively working to improve the situation. There is no magic bullet for improving your body or your mind; you have to *do* the work.

Hypnosis goes against many religious beliefs
There may be some religious practitioners or clergy members in your life and circles that do not approve of hypnosis for lack of understanding. However, there is nothing that hypnosis would require of you that would also require that you violate any of your personal beliefs, philosophies, morals, or comfort zones. When you are being hypnotized, you are simply having suggestions made that will help you to improve situations in your life and, in the case of self-hypnosis, you're making those suggestions yourself so you are in complete and total control of what the outcome is from those suggestions. You do not have to force anything upon yourself that makes you uncomfortable, goes against what you believe, or causes you harm.

Hypnosis isn't an effective means of therapy or help
Everyone is different and you may run into one or more people who are telling you that hypnosis is not a valid form of therapy. That very well may be true for that person, but it doesn't have to be true for you. The only way to know for sure if something will not work for you is to put the work in, do the research into how it works, and see if it's the right fit. There is no one who knows your mind better than you so and there is no one who can look at a therapy or a set of actions of any kind and tell you for certain whether or not it's right for you or how it should make you feel. Many people have experienced real help as a result of self-hypnosis or hypnosis with a professional and there isn't anyone on the planet who is qualified to tell them that they are wrong.

Hypnosis can cure your ails in one session
Not to sound like a broken record about the magic bullet thing, but you have to be willing to give each type of therapy time to work before you decide whether it really is effective. Sure, the high of trying something new and experiencing a deeper sense of consciousness could instill some excitement in you, could get you revved up about getting your mental and physical health in line, but you should give hypnosis about five sessions to make sure that it's doing what it should be doing for you and that it's going the way it should be going. Stay in contact with your therapist or with someone who is experienced in the field and make sure that everything you're experiencing is normal, just to be safe, but give it time and let your therapy do the most it can do for you!

Facts
Some people can't be hypnotized
This is absolutely true. Hypnosis is not for everyone and some people simply cannot make themselves fall into that suggestive state where everything kind of falls into place. The way to know if this is you is that you're just kind of sitting there with the thoughts in your mind and you're not feeling quite relaxed enough. You're not feeling like the things you're saying feel any truer to you, and over time, there is no shift in your subconscious thinking that would lead you to believe that things have changed in your unseen mental process. If you notice that the hypnosis isn't working after a few sessions, contact a therapist and see what other therapies might be considered valid for you and the things that you're hoping to achieve with therapy.

You can't be hypnotized against your will
This is very important. You cannot be hypnotized unless you 100% consent to it. If you're not in agreement with it, it will be impossible for you to relax enough for you to gain any benefits from the therapy. Think about a child who is being told to go to bed when they are not tired. They're going to be hopping

up out of bed every five minutes, thinking about something new that they want or some other reason why they can't get to it right now. Relaxation is an absolute prerequisite to being hypnotized and there is simply no getting around it. Even at the most voracious insistence, you cannot be hypnotized against your will.

You stay completely awake and in control of your cognitive and physical faculties when hypnotized
Being relaxed and being asleep are distinct things that are not mutually exclusive. You should not be asleep during hypnosis or it will not do anything positive for you in the least. Being hypnotized should leave you in complete control of all your bodily processes and your volition. There should not be anything that you can be made to do in your hypnotic state that makes you uncomfortable later and there should not be anything that keeps you from being entirely aware of the conclusions reached and the changes made during a hypnosis session.

Chapter 12: Facts & Myths about Weight Loss

Myths

Weight loss progress can be planned in a straight line
Trying to measure your weight loss in one straight line will often set you up for failure. The body doesn't do anything in one straight line. Progress is something that gains momentum over time and weight loss is something that happens in fits and starts. Try to remember that your weight loss might not be coming along at the rate that you expect, but so long as you keep up on your regimen and you keep your eyes on the prize, the weight loss will come along in due time. Just have faith, keep your focus, stay on the plotted course, and the weight loss will follow.

Carbs make you fat
Carbs do not inherently make you fat. There are different carbs that are of a different quality and picking and choosing what carbs you put into your diet will give you a much more satisfactory result. Having an apple, for example, will serve you much better throughout your day than a serving of chips might. Try your best to get your carbs from fruits and veggies instead of processed snacks and you will find that not only do you get hungry less often and that the carbs stick with you for much longer, but that you get more weight loss over time with those carbs of a higher quality.

Occasional alcohol will stall your weight loss
Having a drink every so often won't knock you out of weight loss mode, so to speak. If you're watching your weight and working on keeping your food and drinks healthy, then the occasional alcoholic beverage when you're out to dinner with friends won't keep you from reaching your goals. You might

find that you need to keep an eye on the number of drinks that you have, but so long as you're not making a habit out of drinking those types of things, you shouldn't experience too much trouble staying on track for healthy weight loss. Cheers to your health!

Cutting the yolk out of your eggs will help you lose weight
The yolks in your eggs have a whole lot of good protein and delicious nutrients in them that could help you to feel great in the mornings. Cutting yolks out of your eggs might not actually provide all the health benefits that people seem to think it does. It's true that there is cholesterol in yolks, but it is a healthy sort that can help you to maintain your health. Eggs are an excellent source of lean protein that can help you to get through your day and to help keep you sustained until lunch.

People with excess weight are unhealthy and people with no excess weight are healthy
Thin people can be unhealthy and overweight people can be healthy. It is true that excess weight can have a negative effect on one's health over time, but it's not guaranteed that one's weight will directly correlate to their health. It is a good idea to monitor your weight and all the indicators of health to make sure you're doing the best you get to keep everything in balance, but it does not serve to think that fat automatically equals lowered health or compromised health. Do your best to stick to a healthy lifestyle and regimen and your health will stay supported throughout.

Eating certain foods will speed up your metabolism
There are a lot of infographics, posts on social media, blogs, and articles backed by pseudoscience that will tell you that certain foods will help you to boost your metabolism. Your metabolism can be boosted with a healthy regimen full of diverse ingredients and nutrients. Eating foods that are rich in fiber, vitamins, minerals, and nutrients will help you to feel your best and it will boost your metabolism by giving it proper

fuel to work with and easy foods to digest. You will not often see an improvement in your metabolism in a short period of time, so keep to your lifestyle and your regimen and you will see those changes coming through over time.

Your workouts have to be intensive for you to lose weight

Many people think that they need to commit themselves to hours in the gym each week so that they can get a jumpstart on weight loss. In reality, running yourself ragged in the gym, spending hours on the treadmill, working hard and pushing your muscles to their limit for long periods of time can have a lot of very negative results. You can hurt yourself, you can burn yourself out, you can give your body too few calories and grams of protein to heal from that work, causing your muscles to suffer in the long and short term, and you can give yourself the impression that exercise isn't worth it. Just like everything else, exercise should come in moderation. 20 minutes of cardio and 30 minutes of other exercise is a great way to keep your body moving, your blood pumping, and your muscles building! Make sure you get plenty of protein, do your stretches, and drink plenty of water and you will do great!

You have to cut out everything in order to lose weight

You don't have to cut every single thing from your diet in order to lose weight. There are a lot of diets out there that glorify cutting out everything that isn't completely organic, everything that isn't plant-based, and so many other things. You don't have to cut out every single component to your meals that you're used to having and you don't have to follow a dietary regimen that isn't sustainable for you. Just cut down on the foods that have less of the good stuff in them and fill in the blanks with lots of healthy, fresh foods that you can enjoy. Having a diet that you can realistically follow for a long period of time is the best way for you to maintain and achieve your weight loss goals.

You have to starve yourself in order to lose weight
Going hungry does not have to be a part of your dietary regimen. Your meals should leave you feeling satisfied and your snacks should give you the pick-me-up you need in order to get through to the next meal. You should feel nourished and full at the end of your meals and you should feel like you've put good fuel into your body. Starving yourself can leave you feeling fatigued, it can cause headaches, and it can even stall your weight loss progress if you're consistently eating fewer calories than your body needs to get through the day. Make sure that your meals are filled with plenty of vegetables and enough protein to keep you feeling your best.

Short-term weight loss diets are effective
This is a myth because short term diets for fast weight loss are called crash diets. They are often damaging to your metabolism and will leave your body confused about how to maintain the weight that you've gotten down to. As soon as you come off that regimen, you're going to pack the pounds right back on and getting them off again is going to be even harder. The best way for you to get sustainable weight loss is to lose it through healthy lifestyle change and to maintain those healthy habits after the weight has been lost. Doing that will allow your body to acclimate to its new life without the excess weight and it will allow your body to handle the occasional indulgence without clinging to all the extra.

Fast food is always fattening
There are some fast foods out there that are working on being more conscious of the health concerns that the public are becoming more and more aware of. Some fast casual places will put menu items up that contain the right amounts of nutrients to help you lose weight while still enjoying food on the go. Be careful about your serving sizes and be sure to look at the calorie counts on the menus when you do go out. You should be able to find plenty of things out there that you can have on the run. And with multiple serving sizes per meal you

buy, you can have the leftovers later so you're getting the most possible bang for your buck!

Slimming pills are a safe way to cut down on your weight.
In many cases, slimming pills contain things that you shouldn't be putting in your body without the advice or supervision of a medical professional. There are pills that can help you to lose weight in a number of different ways and many of them are not good for your body. Some of them will purge all the water weight from your body, some of them will cause you to go to the bathroom a lot, some of them will introduce foreign things to your body that aren't good for you, and some of them just don't do anything at all. Many of them are not safe or effective, so it's best to stick to healthy, practical means of weight loss if you would like to sustain it.

Low-fat or reduced-fat snacks are healthier
Snacks that have that "low-fat" or "reduced fat" label on it are often marketed as the healthier choice for you. Many of those types of foods, however, fill the gap with preservatives, flavorings, and additives that can take away from the healthfulness of the food. In addition to this, there are many products that have no fat in them at all (like marshmallows) that are not healthy for you in any way. Just because they are not made with fat does not mean they are not otherwise made of sugar, carbs, or things that you don't particularly need to be adding to your diet in any large measure. Make sure that the nutritional facts reflect good content in the food that you buy and make sure that you're not focusing on one thing more than another.

Diet sodas are helpful when you're losing weight
Diet sodas can often lead to a larger appetite, making you eat a little bit more than you might otherwise be eating. Diet sodas contain artificial flavors, sweeteners, and colors that can draw you back in a lot of other ways. Aspartame, for instance, can cause headaches when consumed in large measure over a long

period of time. Having a lot of diet sodas in your regimen leaves you with a lot more negative things than you would have if you simply switched to water. Try drinking water with your meals exclusively and then between meals, stick with tea, coffee, or seltzer if you feel the need for some carbonation. This will give you some variety without giving you all that extra stuff that could set you back in the long run.

Eating healthy is enough to lose weight without exercising
If you are eating healthy foods all day long, but you're not making an effort to move your body throughout the day, you will find it much harder to lose weight. Moving your body throughout the day will keep your blood pumping and will burn that fat. You can dwindle a bit simply with diet, but exercise will really make it go the way that it's supposed to and will speed it up. Try keeping your heart rate up for at least 20 minutes per day, then expand from there.

Skipping meals will help you lose weight
Skipping meals in your day will not help you lose weight if you're doing it sporadically. Skipping meals sporadically robs your body of the nutrients it needs, keeps your body from getting used to digesting on a healthy schedule. Having a digestion schedule helps your body to be able to speed up the metabolism and break down foods as they are introduced into your body. If you are going to skip meals, try to do so with Intermittent Fasting, which depends on a specific fasting schedule. This will allow your body to cut down on meals, maximize digestion, and feel its best.

You should just eat less and move more
Telling someone that they just need to eat less and move more in order to lose weight is an oversimplification of the things that could be going wrong and keeping them from losing the weight they wish to lose. Diet and exercise are hugely helpful tools in weight loss, but they might not be the only one that

someone needs in order to experience health and weight loss success. Speak with your doctor if you think these two things might not be working for you and see if you and your doctor can work together to figure out what the missing part of the equation is.

Willpower and not biology is the answer to obesity

Many people make the mistake of thinking that

You must eat breakfast to lose weight
Everyone's body is different, so what someone needs might not be exactly the right answer for someone else. Generally speaking, giving your body protein, carbs, and fiber in the morning is a great way to give yourself a good jumpstart on your day, it wakes you up and gets your body humming. For some people, eating in the morning doesn't help matters, but leaves the body feeling weighed down and sluggish. If this is the case for you, then don't push yourself to have breakfast before your body needs it. You can think of this as an intermittent fast that extends into the late morning. Simply don't eat too many calories at your first meal of the day to over compensate, and make sure that your meals are rich in healthy nutrients that can help your body to feel its best.

Weight loss supplements can help you lose weight without any diet change
There are a lot of supplements out there that claim to be the magic bullets that will help you burn fat like never before. There are supplements out there that claim that just by taking that pill, you can keep your current diet and level of activity and the weight will just fall off of you in no time at all. I am so sorry to have to be the one to tell you that they are all full of bologna. There aren't currently any known substances that can terminate fat in such a targeted and expedient way. The fact remains that diet and exercise are the most effective methods there are for sustainable weight loss.

Weight loss is the same difficulty for everyone
Many people make the mistake of thinking "weight loss is just about getting off your butt and putting the work in. You can drop 5 lbs without really thinking about it, so just do it." Not everyone's bodies are so accustomed to letting go of excess weight, and some people have to work incredibly hard to keep it off. There are lot of factors that can influence one's ability to lose weight and, even though you might think they're niche or rare, they really aren't. Genes and biological components that make weight loss hard are fairly common. There are also genes and biological components that make gaining weight harder. Everyone is different and to assume that any two people would have the same amount of difficulty is largely incorrect.

Exercising a lot means that you can eat whatever you want
Exercising a lot does not mean that you can eat whatever you want. Exercising a ton means that you will get to eat more calories and nutrients than other people around you, but if you simply live off of foods that don't have what you need, then you are going to feel terrible. Working out enough to burn off junk food with no fuel in your body except for said junk food is a catch-22. You won't be able to push as hard because the fuel is subpar. Not being able to push as hard means that you won't be able to work off that junk food. It's best to eat lots of high-quality nutrients that your body can use to get through a nice, medium-difficulty workout on a regular basis. A theme that I'm trying to really convey in this book is consistency. Keeping your workouts and your nutrition consistent will put your body on a low and slow burn that will shed the pounds, keep them off, and help you to feel better than you ever have.

Cutting out gluten will make you lose weight
Gluten does not, in itself, cause weight gain or problems of any kind unless you are allergic to it. The percentage of people with a gluten allergy is quite miniscule and it can manifest itself in a

couple of different ways. If you expect that gluten might be a problem for you, speak with your doctor about getting tested. Now, a way in which eating gluten-free could potentially lead to weight loss is if you cut out bread entirely. Bread can be fattening if you eat a lot of it. It's all carbs and fiber and if it's not balanced well, those carbs can cause a bit of weight gain. Wheat is in a lot of things and, where there is wheat, there is gluten.

Eating gluten-free can also be very fattening, depending on what you choose instead. Rice, corn, and potatoes have no gluten in them, for instance. This leaves a whole host of junk foods at the disposal of someone who is going gluten-free and those aren't particularly great for weight loss either.

If you feel best when you cut wheat out of your diet, then by all means do so. Just be aware that it is not, in itself, and effective means of weight loss.

Losing weight quickly means you will put it all back
This is not exactly true. Losing a bunch of weight with a crash diet, then reverting back to your normal eating habits means you will put it all back. If you are doing something that you can't keep doing forever, like working out for 5 hours per day and eating 500 calories, then you are going to yo-yo when you're done with that regimen. Your body is going to be keeping all the food you put into it for energy for that workout that you're no longer going to have and it's not going to know how to cope with any of it, and the pounds will come right back on.

Healthy food is more expensive
It is common for people to think that healthy foods are more expensive than the ones that are not as good for you. While this is partially true in some cases, there are some things one must consider. Often, when you find expensive healthy food options, they are in restaurants that typically serve other, more hearty, and less health-conscious foods. Those salads and dishes can tend to run a little more pricey because they're not

selling as many of them, and they have to make it worth the costs of keeping those fresh ingredients on hand in their stores and restaurants. In grocery stores and health food stores, you can find that certain goods with particular labels on them such as organic, non-GMO, and farm to table can have a higher price on them because of how they're sourced and transported, and once again to make them worth the price of upkeep. Now, if you want to start making salads at home and you buy:

- One bag of leafy greens - $2.50
- One hot house cucumber, large - $1.00
- One bunch of cilantro - $0.89
- One bag of croutons - $1.00
- One bottle of dressing - $3.29
- One packet of chicken - $5.25
- Two bell peppers - $3.00

This is a total of $16.93 before tax for a week's worth of lunches. Now, even if you go to the dollar menu at fast food restaurants throughout the week and spend $3 before tax on your food, you're still only just breaking even.

Healthy food doesn't have to be more expensive, you just have to know what you're looking for and avoid certain grocery shopping money pits that fancier labels are hoping you will fall into. You can eat healthy on just about any budget, you just have to get practiced at it!

You can sweat excess fat out of your body
You may have heard of people wrapping their bodies in trash bags or sitting in saunas for hours at a time in the hopes that they will sweat out the fat that's in their bodies. This isn't something that can really happen. True enough, working up a sweat does make you burn fat, but that has more to do with the exercise and its rigorousness than the sweat itself.

People have incorrectly assumed, *I lost the most weight when I was sweating like crazy. I must need to just sweat more!* In reality the conclusion they ought to have reached was that they lost the most weight as a result of rigorous exercise that made them sweat more than their other workouts.

Weight loss and fat loss are the same thing
This might sound scary at first, and it can be, but it's fairly easy to make sure you're not going over the line: you can lose muscle mass while exercising if you're not following certain guidelines. Losing muscle makes your weight drop faster than losing fat and you want to make sure that you're not doing things to cause your muscle mass to decrease. Sticking to 20 minutes of cardio is ideal. Doing more than that can start to break down your muscle mass if you're doing that too often. You can also make sure that you're doing strength training along with your frequent exercise because this helps you to build up muscle. The two work together to burn fat, build muscle, and keep you on the right track!

Juicing will help you lose weight
Juicing is not nearly the trend now that it used to be some years ago, but it bears mentioning that it's not the miracle cure everyone seems to think it is. Juicing has a lot of benefits when you juice more vegetables into your diet because you're getting all those nutrients that you wouldn't otherwise be getting if you're unable to eat that many vegetables per day. However, you do miss out on all the fiber that those veggies have to offer and in a lot of cases, people would exclusively juice fruit as opposed to sweetening their vegetable juices with fruit. Fruit juice is delicious and very sweet because it's high in sugar. In most cases, having a glass of orange juice will give you just as much sugar as a candy bar. Upsetting, I know. It turns out that eating fruits and vegetables really is the best way to get fruits and vegetables into your diet.

Food with fat in it makes you fat
Like with carbs, not all types of fat are the same, nor do they have the same effect on your body. The source should often be considered when you're deciding whether or not a type of fat is good for you. The fats from things like nuts, salmon, and

avocados for instance will always be better for you than the fat from potato chips, ice cream, and snack cakes. If you're able to consider the quality of your foods and make sure that you're getting the right kinds of fat. Having a whole avocado every single day might be a little bit much, but healthy fats do have acids in them that your body needs, so don't be shy!

Diet foods will make you thin and healthy
There are a lot of diet foods on the market that are no better for you than their original counterparts. Make sure that you're looking at the label to find out how many carbs, how much sat, how much fat, how much trans fat, how much sugar, etc. By using the nutritional labels and comparing with the standard, you can get a good idea of what foods truly are better for your diet and what foods just want you to think that they are better for your diet.

Simply drinking more water will make you lose weight
Drinking water is a great thing to do for your body. Staying hydrated will avoid a whole host of issues that can make your life harder. Drinking water does ease the weight loss process and it makes it easier for your body to keep up with everything that you're changing in your life. However, simply drinking water without making any other changes to your diet won't get the job done. You need to make sure that you're eating well, sleeping well, and exercising often. Drinking a gallon of water a day without changing anything about your diet or activity level will only make you go to the bathroom more often. Everything else will stay the same!

All calories are created equal
Just like fat and carbs, your calories aren't going to mean the same thing to your body if they're made up of different things. For instance, one tablespoon of sugar is 60 calories. One tablespoon of olive oil is 110 calories. There is quite a difference between these two things, but cooking with a tablespoon of olive oil might be better for you than stirring a

tablespoon of sugar into your morning coffee. Thos calories translate differently because they're made up of different things that your body deals with differently. Make sure you're taking your calories seriously and putting things in your body that it needs.

Facts

Drinking plenty of water makes it easier for you to lose weight
Drinking a lot of water helps your body to keep all its internals lubricated and it keeps things moving along. When your body isn't getting enough water, you will feel sluggish, thirsty, ill, and you might even feel some symptoms that seem like they're out of nowhere. Drinking plenty of water will help you to feel your best when you're making all those changes to your life and if you're exercising, you're going to be purging a lot of moisture from your body by working up a sweat. It's important to make sure that you drink plenty throughout the day, both before *and* after your workouts. Even more ideal is making sure that you're putting electrolytes into your body as well. Salt and potassium are two that you can get in your foods and you can also look to electrolyte supplements to help fill in the blanks wherever they may be.

Eating plenty of fiber helps with digestion and weight loss
Fiber is an excellent thing that comes from fruits and vegetables, as well as other sources. Now, you might be wondering why fiber is so good for you. It's because it's something that your body can't fully digest. I know this sounds counterintuitive, but bear with me. When you eat fiber, it's pushed through your digestive tract, bringing things along with it when it goes. This helps to keep your digestive tract clear and helps to keep you regular. Having troubles keeping yourself

regular can lead to some unpleasantness in addition to retained weight, so fiber is an all-around great idea for your diet!

Having plenty of vegetables is great for weight loss
There are so many reasons for this. The nutrients are wonderful and can make you feel better than you ever have, depending on your past with them. They can keep you feeling regular and healthy. They can fill out a lot of the empty spaces in your meal and they can allow you to feel like you've eaten a very large meal that is in fact very low in calories and very high in nutritional impact. Basically, if you can figure out a place to put vegetables into your diet, you should do it!

Habitually drinking alcohol will cause you to gain weight
We did touch on this in the Myths section of this chapter, but I want to reiterate. While the occasional drink here or there will not stop or stall your weight loss progress, habitual alcohol consumption will absolutely do that. Drinking each day brings a lot more carbohydrates, namely sugar, into your diet. The calorie counts are not typically available on spirits and on alcoholic beverages, though they are not light consumables. They can be quite hefty, especially when mixed with sugary juices and mixers. Just keep a watchful eye and make sure that you're getting plenty of water and good stuff in between each drink, with a good deal of time between as well.

Stress can cause you to retain and gain weight
Stress is a vicious thing that can cause a lot of varied problems in your life. If you are dealing with a lot of stress in your life and you're not dealing with it, it can manifest in so many ways that you might not even believe. One of those ways is weight retention and gain. Feeling stress can also make you lose weight, but not in a way that is sustainable or healthy. Basically, stress is a huge problem for a lot of people and getting rid of it can only serve to vastly improve your life. Look into some stress relief techniques and find some that appeal to you. By using those techniques, you can cut down on your difficulty

with your weight and you can make life a bit more fun, which is always a good idea anyway!

Eating more protein can boost your metabolism

Protein is primo fuel for your body. When you have enough protein in your system, your body has a lot more to work with and can throw its systems into high function. If you are able to put enough protein into your daily meals, you will find that your metabolism is able to work with that fuel and move more quickly, helping you to burn extra calories, keeping from excess fat from forming, and helping you to burn the fat that is already being stored in your body. Try upping your protein and lowering your carbs a little bit at each meal and see what kind of results you get!

Doing more than 20 minutes of cardio each day can break down muscle mass over time

It's important to make sure that you do your cardio each day for about 20 minutes. Exceeding that can have a negative effect on your muscle mass, but this can be counteracted by adding strength training to your regimen. You will find your muscle mass increasing and the fat content in your body lessening while you do this!

Pictures of healthy foods on your refrigerator can often influence you to make better choices

A recent study found that by putting pictures of healthy foods and dishes on your refrigerator, you can influence yourself to have healthier foods when you go hunting for your next meal or snack. Try to find images of colorful, beautiful, fresh foods from magazines or online publications and use them to inspire yourself to put together something that is rich in color, flavor, nutrients, and healthy stuff that your body craves and needs in order to thrive.

Yo-yo dieting can be damaging to your heart health and body
Your heart health could be at risk with lots of yo-yo dieting that causes your weight to plummet and skyrocket over and over again over time. The best and healthiest way is for your body to lose weight steadily over a given period of time, then keeping it off with healthy lifestyle maintenance. Using your self-hypnosis, you can guide yourself to healthy eating habits and relationships with food, then you can keep your weight off, helping your heart and your body to stay in the best possible health.

The more muscle you have in your body, the higher your metabolism will be
Excess fat in the body acts as an encumbrance on your body's ability to do many things. Metabolising the food that you put into your body is slowed when your body is held back by excess fat. When you start to gain more muscle and lose more fat, you will see a significant uptick in your metabolism and in your energy levels. These things are all connected. To build muscle, do strength training and High Intensity Interval Training with strength training focuses throughout and you will see a marked improvement!

Menopause can slow down your metabolism
Menopause can make a significant number of things in your life harder. Weight loss is absolutely one of those things, so don't take it too hard if your weight starts to plateau during that time. Speak with your doctor about things you can do to help with weight loss in spite of everything your body is going through and see if there are any exercises you can do or changes you can make so your body is supported, getting everything it needs, and still losing weight along the way.

Losing weight can improve your brain function and memory

Brain fog is something that can come with the territory of being over-encumbered by excess weight. Many who have lost a significant amount of weight have reported that it's easier for them to think in a straight line, remember things, and keep themselves on task than when they were dealing that excess weight. This is not to say that any amount of fat on your body will make it hard for you to think, but it is a quite interesting phenomenon that excess fat can have an effect on one's mental process!

There are as many as 100 genes that can cause obesity

You may make the mistake of thinking "yes, there are genetic elements that can make weight loss harder, but that's not a very common thing and most people should be able to lose weight with just diet and exercise." There are as many as 100 anomalies in genetics that can make it exceedingly difficult to lose weight, to keep it off, or to keep from gaining it. It's important that you get a feel for your natural proclivity to gain and retain weight and work against it in a healthy pattern that works for your body. If you're not sure of how to do this, contact someone who can work with you on your dieting habits, determine a pattern, and set you on the right track!

Significant weight loss can alleviate arthritis

Arthritis is one of the many illnesses and difficulties in the body that can be exacerbated and greatly aggravated by excess weight loss. Having less weight on the body means that there is less pressure on the joints, less inflammation in the body, and fewer things keeping the arthritis in a flared-up state as often. By losing weight, you can significantly lower your pain levels and increase your ability to manage arthritis and its complications.

Gaining as few as 11 lbs. can slow down your metabolism
Your metabolism is fine-tuned to your body and your weight. Adding extra weight to your body can make it harder for you to feel your best, but many people are unaware of how few excess pounds it takes to make your body slow down and have trouble getting through its daily routines and processes. Paring down your weight is great for confidence, outlook, and self-image, but it's amazing for your health and your well-being as well!

Chapter 13: Frequently Asked Questions

About Weight Loss

How often should I weigh myself?
This is something that is ultimately up to you. You may weigh yourself as often or as rarely as you like, however it is recommended that you take out your scale and look at your weight once per week. Doing this gives your weight time to equalize over the period over several days and you'll get a nice average reading once per week. Make an effort to weigh yourself at the same time on the same day each week. For instance, first thing in the morning after you use the bathroom on Monday will let you know how your week and weekend went. Weighing yourself at the same time of day might seem silly, but doing it when your stomach is empty and when your body hasn't had time to retain any water for the day will give you a nice, even read on your weight and how your progress is coming along without giving you all the fuss of weighing yourself once per day.

Does every one of my meals need to be planned?
In a word, no. It absolutely helps people like myself to have each meal planned so things are never left in the air, left to chance, or left with a possibility of changing to something that I should not be eating. You can plan every breakfast, lunch, dinner, and snack if you are the highly organized type, or if you're someone who likes to kind of go with the flow, you can plan just your dinners and see how that serves you. When all your meals are planned, it keeps the whims of the day and the cravings of the moment from creeping in and helping you to

make decisions that you really ought not be making for the sake of your goals.

Should I skip a meal to compensate for overeating?
Skipping meals in order to overeat at another part of your day is a dangerous practice to bring into your routine. If you eat a lot at one meal, consider still eating, but going lighter at your regular mealtimes. Doing so will allow your body to use the hormones and enzymes it likely has produced in anticipation of the meal you've prepared for it, and it will keep your body well-fed throughout the day. Your body isn't automatically able to hold onto extra calories and disperse them throughout the day as your body needs them. It will use all it can of the meal that you've given it, store the rest, and wait for the next meal to come along and deal with that. Excess fat can come from overeating in a sitting and exercise is really the only way to counteract that overage.

Which fats should I cut back on when dieting?
When trying to cut anything out of your diet, my first suggestion is always going to be for the processed stuff! Remove the fats from your diets that come along with lots of salt, remove the foods that come with lots of saturated fats, and replace them with high fat natural foods like avocados, fish, nuts, seeds, and other such things. You want those monounsaturated fats, the polyunsaturated fats, and you want the fatty acids that come with them. Ditch the chips, ditch the butter substitutes, and ditch the canola oil! Sub in for healthy fruits, fish, butter, and natural alternatives. Doing so will serve you well!

Do I have to keep a food journal?
Just like meal prepping, no you absolutely do not *have* to keep a food journal. Food journals are a helpful tool to bring about accountability as well as a working record of the calories going into your system so you can see where you stand and work your way down from there. You will want to replace the foods

you're eating with healthier versions and you will want to cut down portions when and where you are able to do so without starving yourself or depriving yourself of the essential nutrition your body needs to keep on its merry way. If you feel comfortable with going through your diet without that journal, then you are absolutely welcome to do so.

Can I eat as much grilled chicken as I want?
One of the first things you will want to do when you're committing yourself to a healthy lifestyle is letting go of the idea of "eating as much as you want." Many of us are in the position we're in to seek help with weight loss because of a connection to food that leads us to take more than we need in a sitting. Learning to control your portions when you're dieting is absolutely vital because you are working to retrain your body about the whole concept of food, what kinds of foods it wants, and how much of that food your body should want in a sitting. Whether the food is lettuce, grilled chicken, olives, cheese, or anything else under the sun, ***serving sizes matter.***

How important are calories to weight loss?
Watching your calories is a massive part of weight loss. Your body measures calories, whether you do or not. Weight loss, for a lot of people, is a simple matter of calories in versus calories out. Finding out if this is not the case for you requires that you first take stock of your calories in versus your calories out and determine what you're doing right and what is going wrong. Tracking how many calories you're eating will allow you to cut back or increase wherever it is necessary to do so. Absolutely, it is true that what is in the calories matters just as much as the calories itself, but don't be shy about making sure that you're not eating 300 calories of chicken alone in your dinners. You must leave room for your veggies, carbs, flavorful components, and anything else you wish to add.

What is a metabolism?
Metabolism is a process in the body which turns the food you eat and the things you drink into energy that your body can use. More or less, it is the whole entire digestive process and its speed can very well determine how you feel, how long meals keep you going, how long your meals stay in the body, when you go to the bathroom, and how much of that meal stays firmly planted on your thighs. Speeding up your metabolism means that more gets moved through your body more quickly. The longer a meal takes to work its way out of your system, the higher the chances of it leaving fat stores behind when you're all done with it.

How could genetics affect my weight loss?
The human body is a very complex organism and it is made up of many internal processes, hormones, chemicals, enzymes, etc. There are a lot of genetic anomalies or peculiarities that can keep your body from doing any one of these things in the same way as another person's body. There are so many places in the digestive process where things can go awry, it just presents that many more opportunities for your system to fall flat in one place or another. There are so few people in this world whose bodies operate completely perfectly and even they have some complaint somewhere or another.

Can I keep the weight off after a fad diet?
Long story short, it depends on the fad diet. Many fad diets are predicated on the idea that diets are a temporary regimen to be adopted for a short time, only until the excess weight is eliminated, at which point you can resume your normal habits. In recent years, more things like paleo and keto have marketed themselves like lifetime diets that you can do until the sun goes out, but you have to look at the practicality of those diets, the sustainability of operating on what those diets allow you, either financially, in terms of personal interest, or in terms of nutrition. You have to look at how sustainable all the aspects of it really are and to be honest with yourself about whether

you'd be willing to stay on something like that for the rest of your life. Picking a lifestyle that you like and sticking to it for years at a time is the most effective means of keeping the weight off!

If I am trying to lose weight, should I cut down on fat or calories?
In a word: yes. Cut down on calories absolutely, but don't sacrifice nutrition. Cut down on fats, but keep the monounsaturated and polyunsaturated fats. You want your body to be getting the most bang for its buck when you sit down to eat. You want to feel your best after a meal, you want fuels that your body can use in order to keep you going and to keep you healthy, and you want foods that will keep you close or get you closer to your health and weight loss goals. If you aren't able to feel great when you eat something that is low-fat, then stop eating it! Go for something better. You don't have to settle for foods that make you feel crummy!

How many meals should I eat in a day?
In many cases, you can't go wrong with the classic three squares a day. You can also fill in with little snacks like fresh vegetables and hummus or the like in between if you need. If you are someone who is on the go a lot, who needs a lot of food to keep them going, then you can break your meals into smaller sizes. Eat the same number of calories and the same amount of food overall throughout the day, just broken up into five or six smaller meals throughout the day. Many people find this hard to sustain simply because of the prep and the time it takes to keep oneself on such a schedule. Many people find that three meals and 2 snacks keeps them going without overdoing it.

What is the best exercise routine for weight loss?
This is something that has no one good answer for everyone. Bodies are far too different and varied in their needs and abilities for this to have one good answer. A great place to start,

however, is trying to work in 20 minutes of cardio and 30 minutes of other training or exercise, three days per week. If this isn't something you can manage right off the bat, don't beat yourself up! Work toward it and do what you can and gradually push the limits of what you can do until you expand your abilities and your potential for future workouts. Start your cardio and do five minutes, take a breather, try again, and stop when you feel like you need to. Lift some weights, do some floor exercises, do some stretching and get your body moving. Try a little bit of everything and find the exercises that challenge and leave you feeling like you've just been through a boxing match with Rocky Balboa. You've got this and it will only get better as you keep trying!

How can I control my appetite?
Will power is such a massive part of appetite control for many people. Appetite has taken a back seat to the mental and emotional aspects that have become intertwined into the eating process. If you find that you just can't stop yourself from eating, work on your willpower, work on your affirmations about willpower, and work on your ability to tell yourself no. If you can't, have a trusted friend or loved one help you by telling you no when you need it the most. Outside of being able to say no, you must get yourself used to smaller portions. Cut down your portion sizes little by little if you must, rather than just cutting them in half all at once. Introduce yourself, over time, to a much leaner meal plan and fool your mind into thinking that it's getting everything it wants.

What should I do about cravings?
When you can, ignore them and occupy your mind with something else. Give it 20 minutes. Put your attention on something that is very engaging for 20 minutes, busy your mind, busy your hands, and keep yourself away from an environment with a lot of food in it for that time as well. If, at the end of 20 minutes, you still feel like you need something, find a substitute. Try to have some salted peanut butter with

celery instead of chips. Have some apple slices instead of dessert, have a nice refreshing glass of iced tea, or have something like a piece of hard candy to satisfy your sweet tooth. Those are typically low in calories and in small doses, they should not present a problem for your weight loss goals.

How can I keep the weight off?
As brutal as it sounds, lifestyle change is really the only way. You can't eat two meals a day in your car on the run, you can't spend every single evening on the couch in front of the TV, you can't eat 3,000 calories every single day, you can't keep your body running on four to five hours of sleep a night, and you can't skip meals sporadically and expect your body to just keep up with all of that, keeping you tight, slim, and healthy. You absolutely must make it a point to be active throughout your day, get fresh air, make it a priority to take care of yourself, and do everything in your power to prove to your body that its health is important to you and that it's worth paying attention to. If you're able to do those things and you're able to keep your meal plans healthy by and large, you will find that you don't have a problem with excess weight outside of the holiday season!

About Nutrition

Is 'No Sugar Added' the same as 'Sugar-Free?'

No! No Sugar Added means that they have taken some natural ingredients that already contain sugars and have put them into a product together. Sugar-Free means that the product has been made with synthetic sweeteners that make them safe to consume for people with sugar sensitivity, such as would be found in someone who has Type 2 Diabetes. If you are hoping to get a dessert that won't have a strong impact on your weight and you're avoiding sugar, avoid items that say "No Sugar Added," or at the very least look at the label and make sure that you know what you're getting yourself into. In many cases, synthetic sweeteners should be avoided, but there are times when something sweet would help improve morale and brighten the day.

Has the food pyramid I learned in school been replaced?
Yes, it has! The food pyramid is more or less still a valid guideline for the food groups and what belongs in them, while the guidelines for meal composition have been updated with MyPlate. This is a round chart that looks like a dinner plate, which has been sectioned off for vegetables, fruits, protein, whole grains, and dairy. One quarter of your daily intake should be vegetables. Slightly less than this should be grains, and even less still are fruit and proteins. The smallest portion of your daily intake should be dairy. Using these guidelines can help you put together meals that give your body what it needs without loading you down with dairy your body can't digest and carbs your body can't burn.

How do I know if I have unhealthy eating habits?
Unhealthy eating habits can come in many shapes and sizes. There is no right way to be wrong! If your eating habits leave you feeling sluggish, unhealthy, bloated, or cause you stomach problems, then you may want to make changes. If your meals are sporadic, if you sometimes have popcorn for dinner, if you sometimes find that you can't be sure whether your meals for the day will be well-balanced or mostly carbs, then you will want to make some adjustments so your body can work off of what you're giving it. Eating too little can have just as profound an effect on the body as eating too much can. Eating too little or getting too few nutrients from the food you eat can cause a lot of strange maladies in the body and can contribute to low mood and bad physical health.

What are trans fats and should I avoid them?
Trans fatty acids or trans fats are the fats that come from highly-processed foods. These acids can cause a buildup of bad cholesterol in the body, which can cause difficulties for your

heart and overall health. If you can, avoiding trans fats is a great idea. Eliminating them from your body can prove to be more difficult than purging some saturated fats, and it can have lasting effects as well. Check your nutritional facts labels to see if the indulgent foods you're eating contain these acids. If they do, consider swapping them for something that doesn't contain those acids.

Should I eat every 3 hours or so?
This is a matter of personal preference and need. In many cases, unless you are very active throughout your day, standing, walking, and doing a lot of physical activity, you will likely not need to eat this frequently. However, you can keep snacks on hands like nuts or beef jerky to keep you feeling peppy and ready to tackle your day. If you find that those snacks are not enough, consider breaking your meals into smaller portions and having those more frequently throughout the day.

Where should I look for hidden calories and sugars?
Everywhere. Salad dressings, juices, certain types of flavored water, seasoning mixes, savory baking mixes, prepared canned goods, and so much more. No matter what it is that you're buying for yourself, you absolutely must check the labels. You absolutely must make sure that your foods contain the ingredients and nutrients that you need in your day. If you are trying hard to cut corn starch and excess carbs out of your diet, you will want to check certain seasoning mixes that use that starch as a thickening agent and consider making those same seasoning mixes at home with just spices to get a better result! Keep an eye on the things that you buy and make sure that you're not tripping yourself up along the way to weight loss!

Is fruit juice a good alternative to soda?
Absolutely not. I cannot stress enough that fruit juice is not something you should be working to put back into your daily diet. Fruits should take up such a small portion of your daily intake because they are packed with sugar. Taking out the

dietary fiber from those fruits and then sweetening them up for general consumption will only add to the impact those fruits would otherwise have on your body. If you are looking to replace soda and you are having a difficult time with it, consider switching to seltzer for a short time. Work on bridging yourself over to drinking more water than any other beverage if you do not already do so. Your body needs a great deal of water if it's going to be purging fat each day and drinking soda will only serve to retain that fat for you.

Is all cholesterol bad for me?
No, and depending on who you ask, you might find the sources of good and bad cholesterol to be dubious at best. The rule I like to follow with things such as this is to go with the natural stuff. Eggs, clarified butter, avocados, fatty fish, fatty vegetables, and things that are rich from the earth with cholesterol that doesn't overwhelm your body. Try to make sure that your diet is varied and healthy no matter what you choose and do your best not to overdo it with any one food or another and you will be fine! Your heart health will improve by these means you will feel better and less sluggish during the day as well!

What oils should I avoid?
Avoid oils that are high in saturated fats, avoid oils that come from unnatural sources or which are overly processed, and avoid oils that come from dubious sources. Avocado oil, coconut oil, and olive oil are three great choices that are great for your body and your health in moderation. Things like canola oil, shortening, and vegetable oil are not always the best thing for your body and should often be avoided if you are able to do so!

Should I always stick to organics?
Nope! Thanks to many muddled regulations, the lines between organic and "regular" produce have become blurred and arbitrary. Simply go for the veggies that look fresh and clean! Work within your budget and don't let anyone tell you that

eating the fruits of the earth is a bad idea because it's got the wrong label or price tag on it. What you spend on the foods you eat to sustain and nourish yourself is no one's business but your own and so long as you feel good when you eat your meals, then you don't need to amend anything!

How do I read the Nutritional Facts labels?
The labels on all the foods you buy will tell you some really important things. It will tell you how big a serving size is, how many servings there are in that package (so you know you're getting the best bang for your buck), how many calories are in each serving, and then it will break down the nutrients that are in each individual serving. You will find information on the vitamins, minerals, fats, sodium, carbs, fiber, cholesterol and protein. Some of these things will also be broken down into subcategories so you can make your decisions about whether or not those are the right nutrients for you. You will also find percentages on the vitamins and minerals, telling you how much of your daily value is in one serving. For instance, if your serving of carrots has 203% of your daily value of vitamin A in it, that means that out of the guidelines for typical consumption (based on a 2,000 calorie per day diet), one serving of those carrots has more than double the vitamin A you need to consume each day!

About Health

Are obesity and diseases linked?
Some diseases are linked to obesity, yes. There are often other causes for those same diseases, but obesity can cause many of the risk factors that make those diseases possible. Having excess fat on the body can cause a lot of unseen or unknown inflammation in the body. Because of this inflammation, your body can be weakened or compromised in some places, making it more susceptible to certain illnesses and conditions. The weight itself can also be a direct cause for several illnesses as well. It is also important to note, however, that it is possible

for health to exist in the body of an obese person. Obesity is not immediately a sentence to these illnesses, conditions and diseases.

What can I control about my health with my weight?
By controlling the weight on your body, you can make sure that your health is safeguarded in many ways. For one thing, a thinner body without excess fat can make it easier to spot warning signs, inflammation, and difficulty in the body that might otherwise simply be a product of obesity. Swelling in the feet, for example, can be the indication of something serious for someone who is not overweight. In someone who is overweight, it can simply be water retention, a little too much salt, or general bloating. By controlling your weight, you can keep a close eye on your general health and make sure that you're doing all the things that should be done to keep you feeling healthy and vital.

Are there diets I should avoid for my health?
This should be something that you discuss with your doctor. Your personal health may dictate that you do things a little bit differently for your health than someone else might want to do for theirs. For instance, if you don't feel quite as well when you take on a lot of fat in your diet, you would want to avoid a diet like keto. Keto focuses on having plenty of healthy fats to use as fuel so it can work to burn the fat in your body constantly. If you don't do well on a diet that is devoid of animal proteins, then you won't want to go vegan! Talk with your doctor about the most ideal type of diet and make sure you're doing what works for you.

Are there types of diets that can damage my health?
Certainly there are. You don't have to have a medical degree to write books about what people should be eating. This means that there could be diets out there that are predicated on complete fabrications of science and chemistry, and which dictate that people eat only very little of foods that would

actually nourish them. There are some trends and diets that go with them that could leave you feeling terrible and which are just a couple of steps short of an eating disorder in and of themselves. Don't fall for those; make sure you do your research with plenty of sources and do what is best for your own body and which makes sense to you and to your doctor.

How can I spot a vitamin deficiency?
There are a lot of ways in which your body can manifest vitamin deficiencies. This is largely due to the fact that there are quite a large number of vitamins and each of them affects something different in your body. If you are feeling strange or off, dfo an internet search with "[symptom] vitamin deficiency" and see what comes up! It's very important to make sure you put vitamin deficiency in your search because otherwise the results that come up could be needlessly hair-raising! It can also help to take a daily multivitamin with your breakfast to fill in the blanks! Even the healthiest diets can be missing things here and there.

How can I make sure I'm getting everything I need from my meals?
Follow the MyPlate guidelines and make sure you're looking at the nutrition labels for the foods you eat. Any foods that don't have such labels can be researched online and the information can be supplied that way. Make sure that your meals are varied; don't eat the same exact salad for lunch every single day. Change up your veggies, your recipes, your proteins, and your choices in the kitchen and you will change things up enough that your body is keeping up with what it needs between that and your daily multivitamin.

How can weight loss make me healthier?
By losing the excess weight on your body, you will be cutting down on inflammation in the body, you will be introducing plenty of healthy habits and nutrients, you will be getting your body active and moving, you will be getting plenty of sunlight,

and you'll be getting your daily nutrients as a matter of course. All of these things together will contribute to a much greater personal health and will help you to feel better than you have ever felt before. In addition to this, you will find more activities and foods that you like in your travels, which you can continue to maintain, which will not only get you to your healthiest, they will keep you there!

Am I unhealthy because I am overweight?
Speak with your doctor if you think your weight could be contributing to a health concern for you. It is not so cut and dry as "fat = unhealthy," however excess weight on the body has been known to cause a great many difficulties for people. It is so much easier to maintain one's health if the body is well-maintained. If you are able to lose the weight in a healthy way, keep it off, and to keep yourself on an active regimen with lots of high-quality nutrients, then you will find that you feel better than you ever did when you were lugging around those extra pounds.

About Self-Hypnosis

Does self-hypnosis hurt?
Absolutely not. There is nothing about the hypnosis process that should cause you any pain of any kind. Your goal when getting into a hypnotic state is to lie back or sit back in a position that makes you very comfortable, and then to relax as thoroughly as you possibly can. You will want to focus on the muscles in your body, from the top all the way down to the bottoms of your feet and make sure that they are letting go of and releasing any held tension so you can fully relax and slip into that state of subconscious suggestion.

Is it possible for me to mess up my mental health with self-hypnosis?
No. Absolutely not. When you are doing self-hypnosis, you are simply fully relaxing yourself, putting yourself into that state of

subconscious awareness, and putting affirmations and suggestions into place that will allow you to let go of the difficulties that are holding you back in life. The only way to mess up your mental health in this state would be so unachievable, the thought might even seem laughable. You are only going to be telling yourself what you need to hear. You are worth it, you can do this, you have got this, and your success is assured are the types of things you will be telling yourself and I simply can't see how that could be damaging to your mental health.

Can I overdo it?
The only way to overdo self-hypnosis would be if it got in the way of your other pursuits, routines, or endeavors. You can do self-hypnosis as often as you feel is necessary or helpful to you, and you can cover the suggestions that speak to you most. Outside of those parameters, you shouldn't have any trouble finding a schedule and a routine that works best for you. Try to keep a regular schedule and try to use it as a tool to keep you on track when you need it! If you find that things are getting a little bit difficult and you would like to use self-hypnosis as a way to bring some perspective and to calm you down, that can also be a very helpful tactic!

How often should I do it?
As often as you are comfortable with doing it. You can start with once per week to make sure that you're keeping up regularly with it and if you feel like you need to increase or decrease from there, you are absolutely free to do so. Not having to count on a therapist's schedule or traveling to a professional office can make the therapy so much more accessible and easy to attain, making help that much closer to you. Simply pick your schedule and have at it!

Can I use self-hypnosis for things other than weight loss?
Absolutely you can! Weight loss is what we're covering in this book, but as I have mentioned time and time again throughout

these chapters, you are putting yourself into a subconscious state, which makes you receptive to suggestions and affirmations. Tell yourself that you're good enough for that promotion at work, tell yourself that you are enough, tell yourself that you are going to seize every single moment because you can, tell yourself that you are worth the effort in life. Whatever areas of your life you would like to achieve, consider doing some affirmations about them and see what differences you can make!

Is it dangerous?
The only danger in self-hypnosis would be if you happened to leave something in the oven while you're doing it. It's a very relaxing, low-risk, low-stakes therapy that has a very high reward. If you are concerned for your safety when you're doing this therapy, consider letting someone know that you're doing it and have them look in on you quietly throughout the process so they can help you with anything that might come up along the way!

What does it feel like?
It feels a lot like meditation. It feels like you're resting comfortably in a position, like you're concentrating on a specific goal or purpose, and like you're aligning your thinking to allow you to achieve that goal or purpose. If you feel floaty while you're doing your self-hypnosis, that could be your more whimsical side delighting at the mental weight that you're lifting from yourself. You might even find that you feel a little bit lighter around the shoulders if some particularly stressful subject works itself out for you. These are all natural and exactly what you should hope to gain from your regimen!

Can I get stuck in hypnosis?
Think back to when you were a child and your mother told you that if you continued to cross your eyes or make an ugly face, you would get stuck that way, unable to bring it back to its normal state. Think back on that statement now and realize

how silly that sounds to you. This is also the case for hypnotism and you cannot get stuck in that state any more than you can fall asleep and stay that way or stay drunk forever. These states of mine and subconsciousness are temporary *always* and what you do with your thinking in the time you spend in these states is entirely up to you, and will not affect their duration.

Are there words that I should use over others?
Yes. You should use the words and the phrases that make the most sense to you. If you find an affirmation or suggestion that simply doesn't ring the right bells for you and there is a subtle rewording that might work better for you, use that instead! Even if it's a complete rewrite, go for it! For instance, you might find *You are a warrior queen who can achieve anything she wants*, but you are neither a warrior nor a queen in your mind, you can change it to something like *You are a strong and capable person with much to offer. Your goals are within reach right now.* Or any other phrase that strikes true in your heart. It must give you a feeling and you must identify with it for it to work, so pick good ones!

Chapter 14: Living Your Best Life

Basic Nutrition

Learning about various dietary programs and regimens shows you a lot about how the body works and a lot of ways in which you can change some very basic things about your routine. One of the things that might slip through the cracks is a word to address what a "normal" diet should typically look like in order to promote physical health and fitness. When I say health and fitness, I don't mean Mr. Universe and Ms. America. I mean your average, healthy person who doesn't have too many concerns with their health and who is reasonably active from day to day.

The most basic nutrition should cover all your needs. It should keep you going through your day without making you feel lulls and crashes. It should give you all the energy you need without leaving you with too much extra food to create excess weight on your body. When you're getting the right things in your diet and in the supplements that you're taking, you should have enough energy to get up and get moving from time to time throughout the day and you should have some energy at the end of the day to do more of the things that are important to you in life.

Now, there are other reasons why one might get through the day and feel like there is no way to summon the energy or interest to do the things that typically excite you. If you firmly believe that your nutrition is completely sound and that your body is being sustained, yet you still feel like you can't summon the energy or interest to get involved in the things that are typically quite important to you, there could be some mental reasons behind that. Stress and depression can make it very difficult to engage in the activities we know we love and they can rob you of the energy you would normally have to do them.

Just in case you're unfamiliar with what a "normal" diet should look like and how you can best provide a balance for your body to use to thrive, I'll break it down here in this chapter. This isn't a diet, this isn't a way to lose weight unless you're currently overeating, and this isn't a diet that is low-carb, low-fat, or revolutionary in any way. This is the basic diet that most adults (there are absolutely exceptions, so please adhere to the things you know to be right for you and your needs) can adhere to for a decent balance in their day.

Healthy Habits

There are plenty of healthy habits you can adopt into your daily routine to help you to gravitate toward health with each passing day. In the grand scheme, it might seem like a lot of habits to have to adopt all at once. The key is to just start trying to work toward two or three habits at a time until they become automatic, then gradually add more habits over time. Health is not a static thing and it requires constant maintenance and the constant use of healthy habits.

The best healthy habits are the ones that can become comfortable for you over time. The ones that are too lofty and unrealistic will only leave you feeling defeated. Try not to aim for goals that are a drastic change from where you start. If you want to ultimately drink 96 ounces of water in a day (more than the daily recommended average), but you currently struggle to get 16 ounces into your day, start by aiming for something easier like 32 ounces. This is still less than you should be drinking, but it's easier to obtain. Be realistic with yourself about your current habits and where you ultimately want to end up. Doing so will allow you to set intermittent goals and benchmarks for yourself that will get you where you want to be.

Here are some great healthy habits it's great to adopt into your life over time!

- Walk for 30 minutes each day.

- Exercise for 30 minutes, three days out of every week.
- Drink 64 ounces of water each day.
- Eat 2,000 calories or fewer per day.
- Eat from each of the five essential food groups each day, favoring fruits, vegetables, and lean proteins.
- Sleep for six to eight hours each night.
- Cut down on the stress in your life.
- Relax when you're not at work and put your mind on the things that you enjoy and which help you to feel at ease.
- Take at least one day each week when you have no obligations.
- Connect with other people and relate to them.
- Don't eat at restaurants more than once per week.
- Take up hobbies or activities that minimize stress and which allow you to feel at peace.
- Stand up from your desk at work once an hour and take a lap.
- Stretch throughout the day to keep your joints and muscles from getting too stiff.
- Fill your plate halfway with fruits and/or vegetables, then use the rest of the plate for the denser, more calorie-heavy foods.
- Change up your meals so you're not always eating the same thing at each meal. Variation is a helpful key to a healthy diet.
- Find time to disconnect from things like social media and the outside world. Make a space that is comfortable for you, doing the things you enjoy from time to time.

Your Physical Health

Staying physically healthy is something that a lot of us are working toward, and it can be a little bit daunting. Some of us have complex medical histories that dangle certain conditions over us like a Sword of Damocles. Keeping healthy can be a taller order for some than for others.

There is a very large number of people who are battling things like genetic illnesses, autoimmune disorders, obesity, both types of diabetes, and so many other illnesses that can make a seemingly typical and gradual approach to health feel like it's impossible. It's important to stay in contact with your doctor if you're one of the people with more health concerns than most. Make sure that you're following all of your doctor's recommendations for your personal health and make sure that you're not adopting habits that they wouldn't recommend for you or that they recommend against.

Keeping yourself from getting sick can feel like a battle you're never certain that you're winning. Simply follow the guidelines for basic health as best you can and get medical advice for the rest if you have other health concerns. When it comes to taking gambles, your health is the last thing you need to compromise. For many of us in the world, our health is taken for granted. We eat junk food, pull late nights, treat coffee like a meal, smoke cigarettes, eat donuts for breakfast, and do plenty of other things to put our physical health at risk because it satisfies an immediate want or need. It's important to watch habits like that and make sure that they're occasional at best and that you don't make habits out of them. If you have already made a habit out of them, it's not too late to put a stop to it and to put healthy habits and mechanisms in their place.

Take a look at the list in the previous section and pick out a few of those habits that make you think, "It would be really neat if I could consistently do that," and start working toward it. Treat yourself like a project, if that helps your perspective. Make habitual moves in the right direction and eventually, you'll have a routine that's above reproach by medical professionals and your health will be much more secure than before.

Physical Activity

Getting a decent amount of physical activity in your day is a great way to keep your health in order and it's a great way to break up the flow of your week to bring in a little bit of excitement. The types of activity you put into your week are entirely up to you and your decisions should be based on the kinds of things that you like to do and which you can start to get excited about.

If you're like me, the excitement was never one of the words I would have used to describe myself when it came to the topic of physical activity. However, you can find things that you enjoy, or you can create ways to get enjoyment out of the physical activity that you're doing. In this section, I'll list a lot of different physical activities you can do and I'll go into some creative ways to make them a little more enjoyable or rewarding.

It's important that you don't see physical activity and exercise as a punishment or as a form of torture. Physical activity is a wonderful way to make sure that you're keeping your blood moving, you're working off any extra calories that you've taken in over the week, and that you're getting some time in the fresh air and the sun if that's possible.

Did you know that sunlight provides vitamins for the human body? By putting yourself in the sunlight, you can get both vitamins D and K in amounts that make a difference over time. There are supplements you can take, but missing out on this particular method of delivery for them can have unfortunate side effects on the body and can even lead to you feeling weak or to you having a weakened immune response.

Take a look at this list and see if there are any activities that stick out as things that you would like to try by yourself or with friends to keep your body moving and to keep your blood pumping!

- Aerobics
- Badminton
- Ballet
- Ballroom Dancing
- Baseball
- Basketball
- Bicycling
- Breakdancing
- Canoeing
- Cross-Country
- Diving
- Elliptical
- Football
- Frisbee Golf
- Gardening or Yard Work
- Golf
- Hiking
- Hip Hop Dancing
- Interpretive Dance
- Jogging
- Jumping Rope
- Kayaking
- Martial Arts
- Ping Pong
- Pop and Lock
- Power Walking
- Relay Races
- Running
- Scavenger Hunts
- Soccer
- Softball
- Spelunking
- Surfing
- Swimming
- Tennis
- Ultimate Frisbee

- Urban Exploration
- Volleyball
- Walking
- Wall Climbing or Rock Climbing
- Yoga

Things to increase your enjoyment of these activities:
- Talking with a friend
- Thinking about creative pursuits
- Listening to music
- Listening to podcasts
- Listening to audiobooks
- Meeting up with friends to play
- Watching television if you're running or walking on a treadmill or using an elliptical

When you can turn your physical activity time into time that you spend doing things you enjoy alongside that activity, you will often find that it's not as hard to get yourself into the swing of things again. It's hard to force yourself to get back into the gym when the only thing you got out of going in the first place was sweat and pain! Do some things that allow you to feel a reward or enjoyment in the time you're investing in your personal health.

There aren't any right or wrong answers when it comes to getting active. What gets your body moving and what helps you to have a great time doing it is what matters. If you find that you kind of like bicycling, but you wish there was a little bit more novelty and physical challenge to it, consider getting a unicycle. If you like to do aerobics, but you like the idea of having a lot of music to it, consider dance aerobics. If you like to travel through the city and look at abandoned sites so you don't even feel like you're exercising, UrbEx (Urban Exploration) is a great way to go (just make sure you're not breaking any laws and that you're keeping yourself safe.)

The world is a wonderful and exciting place and there are lots and lots of things you can do to keep your blood pumping and to keep you excited while you do that. Just keep looking for ways to get active and have fun with it!

The Immune System and Nutrition

Your immune system, as I'm sure you're aware, helps you to fend off illnesses that could harm your body. When potentially harmful things come into your body, your immune system sends antibodies to attack those things to keep them from disrupting (or damaging) the systems inside your body. Sometimes the immune system wins and sometimes it needs some help from medicine or other medical procedures.

Your immune response is boosted or hindered by a bunch of different factors that are present throughout your life. When you're not getting enough sleep, your immune system isn't as active as it could or should be. When you're stressed out, the hormones that your body produces can throw off your immune response. When you're not eating the right foods, your body might not have the fuel it needs for the immune system to take care of things the way it needs to.

Making sure that your body has everything that it needs is a good way to make sure that your body is prepared for anything that might come its way. Getting decent amounts of sleep, getting proper nutrients, taking vitamins and supplements to give your body everything it needs, cutting down on stress, keeping yourself from starving, and keeping your general physical health in line are all essential parts of ensuring that your immune system is prepared to fight off any viruses, bacteria, or contaminants that could cause health issues for you.

There are plenty of foods you can add into your diet that will make it easier for your immune system to thrive. Take a look at this list and think about some ways you could work them into your regular diet for a healthier immune system!

- Almonds
- Beans
- Bell peppers
- Brazil nuts
- Broccoli
- Cherries
- Citrus fruits
- Garlic
- Ginger
- Green tea
- Green veggies
- Kiwi
- Papaya
- Pomegranate
- Poultry
- Pumpkin seeds
- Sardines
- Shellfish
- Spinach
- Strawberries
- Sunflower seeds
- Sweet Potatoes
- Turmeric
- Walnuts
- Yogurt

As you can see from this list, there are quite a few different types of foods from various food groups that you can put into your routine to help your immune system to get everything it needs. It's important to keep your protein, adequate numbers of carbohydrates, and adequate vitamins and minerals coming through your system on a consistent basis so you can make sure that you're keeping your body as possible as you can.

The next time you go grocery shopping, see how many of these immune-boosting foods you can work into your menu for the week so your body is getting the best possible defense against things during cold and flu season, and against anything else that might come your way. You never know just what kinds of things your body will come into contact with, and the only way to make sure you're prepared for them is by keeping your health supported all year round!

When it comes to your health, working to undo the damage an illness can do is much harder than it is to take the preventive measures necessary to fight them off. This is where we get the phrase, "An ounce of prevention is worth a pound of cure." Doing just a little bit to make your body more adequately prepared to fight things like the common cold and the flu can keep you far more comfortable than even the most effective cures, as your body still has to fight to get rid of that once it makes its way in.

Luckily enough, it's some of the most delicious foods that nature has to offer which provide some of the most key nutrients for proper and adequate immune response. Bell peppers, shellfish, citrus fruits, and poultry are foods that are quite common in the diets of many people. Think of some ways you can work a little bit more of these types of foods into your lunches, into your snacks, and think of some of the less healthy foods that you could replace with these to really make a big difference in your body's fitness against illness!

Hydration's Role

Drinking enough water is something that is getting a fair amount of attention these days. There are a lot of people who aren't sure if they're getting enough water, and there are some people who may be drinking too much water without even realizing it. It turns out that being properly hydrated can make a world of difference in a lot of different areas of your body and even in your mental clarity.

When your body starts to dry out, systems in your body can't run as smoothly or as efficiently. Think of it like giving your body an oil change! Water quite literally lubricates different areas of your body and allows them to work with one another to carry out the most primary and essential functions in the body. From sleeping well to managing stress, there isn't one process of the body that isn't made easier by having an adequate amount of water in your system and the proper electrolytes to help that water make it into the places where it's supposed to be.

The daily recommended average for water intake is about 64 ounces per day. That's eight glasses of water throughout the day at eight ounces each. Some people will try to go for gold and force an entire gallon into their body in one day and they're left rushing to the bathroom all day long. A gallon is twice the daily recommended value (128 ounces) and it could be too much for your body. You should be drinking enough to keep you from being thirsty and you should be drinking enough that you're going to the bathroom a few times per day, but not often enough to be considered excessive.

Many people have found a happy medium somewhere between 64 and 96 ounces of water per day, taken at about eight ounces at a time. If you're drinking 96 ounces of water per day, that's 12 glasses of water a day, which might seem like a lot. Just like with any of the other healthy habits described in this chapter, this is something that you should pursue with a gradual approach. Drink a little bit more water throughout the day and, eventually, you will find that it will occur to you more naturally to do so.

If you're like me and don't have time to be running to the bathroom every 10 to 20 minutes because you're trying to drink enough water, then I have a little bit of a tip to share with you. The human body takes 15 minutes to absorb eight ounces of water. Think of your body like a dried out house plant. If you pour a whole watering can right onto the plant, it's going to overflow and go everywhere. However, if you do a nice, slow pour or if you pour a bit, wait for it to sink into the soil, then pour again, you can get much more water to absorb into the soil for the plant.

So, try to mark your water bottle at the eight-ounce marks or use an eight-ounce cup to limit your intake to that. Of course, if you're thirstier and want more than eight ounces, you're absolutely welcome to have more. Spacing out your drinks in this way could simply help you to avoid excess trips to the bathroom, spending more money on toilet paper and your water bill, and it could certainly save you time throughout the day.

If you simply don't remember to drink water because of your busy schedule, you're not alone. There are loads and loads of people in the same boat as you. Try leaving yourself little sticky note reminders, setting alarms in your phone, or asking a friend to occasionally remind you to take a little drink here and there. You would be shocked what a difference this makes and how for it goes to keep you looking and feeling your best!

Those who drink enough water are more likely to fight off illness, to have an easier time with weight loss, to have an easier time getting to sleep, and to get less exhausted in the middle of the day. It might sound crazy, but drink enough water for a couple of weeks and notice how much clearer your skin is, notice how much better you feel, and bask in your own glow!

The Quality of Your Nutrition

We've talked a lot in this chapter about the numbers of calories and we've touched a little bit on the quality of the nutrition in your body. It's important to talk about how vital proper nutrition can be to the body and how essential it can be for one's overall health, clarity, and quality of life. There is a school of thought that is floating in the world of Dietetics that it doesn't so much matter *what* you're eating, as it does *how much* you're eating. Others in this field heartily disagree and say that it has nothing to do with how much you eat, so long as the food you're eating is high enough quality. It turns out that both of these ideologies have a bit of validity, and they also have some flaws in their logic as well.

As it turns out, both of those things matter. What you're eating matters almost just as much as how much you're putting into your body. You want to make sure that you always remember to keep your calories in and your calories out in balance if you're trying to maintain, while also maintaining proper nutrition, a good mix of your food groups, and a good quality of the foods that you're eating. Certain foods can fall into the various food groups and still be a little bit lower quality. For instance, you might see some applesauce that has been jarred with sugar, flavorings, and preservatives added. This, when compared to simply eating an apple pales in quality. Your body will get far more from that single, raw apple than it will from that jar of processed applesauce.

It's important to make sure that you're getting plenty of raw fruits and vegetables in your diet like salads, fruits, sliced veggies to snack on, and things of this nature as well as the good, cooked stuff. Certain foods that have been processed and packaged are not bad for you, but one should avoid trying to live solely on things like crisps and crunchy snacks made from vegetables.

There are a couple of things you can pay attention to as a way to give you the reassurance that you have chosen the right foods for your body and your health. The first one is to check the ingredients list. Look out for the names of chemicals, dyes, preservatives, fillers, and other ingredients that you wouldn't put into a food while cooking yourself, or ingredients that can't be acquired without a commercial license. If you need special chemical handling staff in order to add them to your dishes, you likely don't need to be eating them!

The ingredients list will often have things broken down and you'll see things listed with [chemical name] (added for coloring). Make sure that the item being named isn't something that could be less than healthy. Certain health foods will use things like beets and turmeric for coloring because they're very powerful colorants. Things like this are perfectly fine.

You will sometimes see people saying things like, "If you can't pronounce it, you shouldn't be eating it," which is hogwash. There are plenty of foods that come from all different parts of the world with unique and seemingly odd names that are perfectly fine to consume. Simply do your research on what the ingredients in your foods are and educate yourself realistically on their effects on the body and digestion. Your own curiosity and peace of mind are the only things you're trying to satisfy here, so set your own standards for the foods you will eat and don't compromise on them.

When you're planning your meals for the week, make sure that processed foods and snack foods are used only in moderation and try to get an abundance of lean proteins, healthy dairy products if you're into dairy, lots of fresh produce, and delicious flavors from all over the world to breathe life into your dishes. Eating healthy is no fun if it doesn't taste good, so try out lots of spices and sauces to make your dishes the best they can be!

Achieving Balance

Achieving balance in your life is often easier said than done. It's not something that makes a whole lot of sense to people until they experience it for themselves. For many of us, there is no bringing balance into our lives. Life is what it is, we roll with the punches, take the twists as they come, and adapt to them the best ways we can. This is a recipe for utter disaster across the board in life and it leaves far too many openings for more stress, confusion, and difficulty to seep into our lives without warning.

Balance is achieved in life by insisting that we achieve it. There is no way that you can simply ask for balance in your life and have it dropped into your lap. It doesn't work that way and, even if it did, it wouldn't be balanced for you because everyone's idea of balance is unique. It's up to you to evaluate the things in your life that are out of balance, the things that are in balance, and to bring everything into proper proportion and order so that you're living the best way you possibly can. While I mean this for life in general, it is just as important when you're talking about diet.

When we talk about a balanced diet, we're not saying, "Eat equal amounts of everything all the time." This isn't how a balanced diet works because certain things can outweigh each other nutritionally. What we mean by balance is having enough of each type of food group to represent it without going too far out of moderation.

You must have enough fruits and vegetables to account for about one half to two-thirds of your daily intake. Doing this provides your body with excellent roughage, delicious nutrition, and enough bulk that you feel full at the end of each meal. Imagine if half of your entire lunch was vegetables. Salad greens, herbs, mushrooms, bell peppers, onions, tomatoes, and maybe come cucumbers with a little bit of chicken and maybe some sprinkled cheese. That salad is going to be delicious and filling and you're going to feel totally full at the end of it.

Occasionally, you're going to want to indulge in a meal that you wouldn't normally consider proper nutrition. This is fine, so long as it's occasional. The ideal for this would be no more than once a week. Try to pick places that are still largely healthy for you where you can get diverse food groups in your meal, but I know there will be times when you're just hankering for something like a fast-food burger or burrito, which is fine. We're all human and we're all allowed to indulge from time to time. Just know that doing that too frequently could be more damaging than rewarding in the long run. You're worth more than regular trips to the fast-food place, and you shouldn't have to sacrifice your health for them!

If you're having trouble switching away from eating out at restaurants all the time to cooking more at home, try a gradual approach! Doing too much at once could be a shock to your routine and it could make it difficult to settle into something that would work better for you in the long term. Try cooking at home four nights a week and try bringing your lunches with you to work. See how this serves you and try to work in more cooking of your own as time goes on.

You might find that, if you're a particularly busy person who doesn't have time each day to prepare breakfast, lunch, and dinner for yourself, that meal prep is right for you. Consider taking time on one night a week to make your breakfasts, lunches, and dinners ahead for the week so you can easily grab and go!

Living Your Best Life

Living your best life is all about doing the things that are right for you. It's about making sure you're eating the right foods, it's about making sure that you're getting enough enjoyment in your life, it's about making sure you're not crushed by the stress of everyday life and of working full time, it's about keeping yourself from missing out on the things that make life worth living, and it's about making the most of your time with the people who matter the most to you. For a lot of people in this world, there are heaps and heaps of obstacles that keep them from achieving these things and there are always reasons why they can't be supported or done.

Living a life that brings you joy and that fulfills you isn't easy. It takes a lot of time, it takes a lot of effort, it takes a lot of dedication, and it might not even feel like it's fun sometimes, but it's all worth it and it's all about the long term. You're here in this world to enjoy a life of your own making and you're here to do more than enjoy foods that will shorten your time with the people who make life worth living.

Do yourself a favor and work more foods into your diet that will help you to not only prolong your time here, but add more tenacity, verve, and passion into the time that you have here. Eat more of the things that will make you feel like you can do anything. Eat more of the things that will help you feel ready to go out and face the world head-on, and do so without wishing that you were eating something that did the opposite. We're all human and to have cravings from time to time is perfectly normal and natural. All I'm saying is that when those cravings hit you and make you feel like you should just abandon the pursuit of foods that will improve your health, remind yourself of what those foods are really good for. Remind yourself of the things those foods can cause for your body, and remind yourself of how you feel when you're on a steady diet of them. Chances are, you won't find them so appealing when you're brutally honest with yourself about those things.

The next time you find yourself thinking about how great it would be to order out for a second time in a week, think about paying for that order with a few minutes of happiness. That's a few minutes of happiness you won't ever get back, because you spent them on greasy foods that don't help you reach your goals. They suddenly seem less worthy of the time and expense, don't they?

You're worth so much more than that and you can't put a price on your own happiness. Let's have a toast to you and the life of balance that awaits you!

Recipes for Healthy Living

I wanted to include some of my favorite healthy recipes with you, dear reader, as a way of complimenting your journey and leaving you with something *actionable* that you can do as soon as you finish this book! For each recipe, I have explained when the most optimal time would be to consume this meal, depending on digestive health.

If you are gluten intolerant, plant-based, lactose intolerant, or vegetarian, every animal or gluten-based ingredient can be replaced with its vegan/gluten-free counterpart. These recipes are delicious and are the main way I now maintain a healthy figure. They are nutrient-dense, tasty, varied, and easy to make. Whether you have never cooked in your life, or whether you fancy yourself a bit of a chef, I am sure that you will enjoy these meals as much as I have.

Breakfast Recipes

Strawberries and Cream Oatmeal:

Here's a recipe from self-confessed oatmeal fanatics, *Fit Foodie Finds*. Ever wake up craving something fresh, summery, and sweet? This is your answer. Lee Funke, founder of *Fit Foodie Finds* recommends using coconut cream as a lighter alternative to heavy cream. This recipe is also vegan, but you can use dairy milk and products if you prefer.

Ingredients:

- 2 cups rolled oats
- 2 cups chopped strawberries
- 2 Tbsps. chia seeds
- 1 medium banana mashed
- 1 tsp. vanilla extract
- 4 cups unsweetened almond milk
- 2 Tbsps. maple syrup

Method:

- Place all ingredients into a medium pot and bring to a boil over medium/high heat, stirring often.
- Once boiling, turn down to low and continue cooking for around 10 minutes or until thick and creamy. Make sure to continue stirring throughout the entire process.
- Top with more berries, chia seeds, and coconut cream. (Funke, March 2020)

Blueberry Peach Oatmeal:

This one's for all you Southern belles, or anyone who appreciates a peachy summer breakfast. This recipe contains healthy fats and protein that will leave you feeling full and energized after fasting. These oats are topped with ground flax seeds and a spoonful of natural peanut butter. Peanut butter is one of my favorite things to add into any oatmeal recipe. It also helps balance out the sugars with the fruit. Brittany Mullins, original recipe writer for this dish, uses almond butter instead. Any nut butter will work with these flavorings.

Ingredients:

- ½ cup old fashioned oatmeal
- 1 cup water
- 1 cup fresh peaches chopped into small chunks and divided
- ½ cup fresh blueberries divided
- ½ tsp. vanilla extract
- ¼ tsp. cinnamon
- ½ Tbsp. ground flaxseed
- 1 Tbsp. peanut butter or other nut butter

Method:

- Add oatmeal, water, ½ cup peaches, ¼ cup blueberries, vanilla and cinnamon into a small saucepan.
- Cook over medium heat for 5-10 minutes or until oatmeal has thickened and is the consistency you like.
- Spoon into a serving bowl. Top with remaining peaches, blueberries, ground flaxseed and nut butter. Enjoy! (Mullins, March 2021)

Brittany Mullins's recipe notes:

Fresh peaches and blueberries work great during the summer, but feel free to use frozen fruit in the winter. Just thaw the fruit and follow the recipe as normal. (Mullins, March 2021)

Fall Spiced Apple Cranberry Oatmeal:

A warm bowl of spiced apple *anything* is tasty enough to get you out of bed in the morning. This is a great oatmeal recipe to keep you fuller for longer and also tastes unbelievably good.

Ingredients:

- ½ cup rolled oats, quick or old fashioned can be used
- ½ cup unsweetened almond milk
- ½ cup water
- ⅛ tsp. (heaping) cinnamon powder
- 1 pinch nutmeg
- 1 pinch ginger
- 1 pinch salt
- 1 tsp. packed brown sugar
- ½ of a medium apple, diced
- 1 Tbsp. chopped raisin cranberry blend
- 1 ½ tsps. coconut cream

Method:

- Add the oats, almond milk, water, cinnamon, nutmeg, ginger, and salt to a microwavable bowl and stir in together.
- Cook in the microwave on HIGH power for 2-3 minutes. At 1 ½ minutes, stir the mixture and ensure that it doesn't overheat.
- Stir in brown sugar, apples, and raisin blend.
- Allow to cool, then drizzle top with coconut cream. Add a tablespoon or two of unsweetened almond milk to top with. (optional)

Cherry Almond Oatmeal:

Ingredients:

- ½ cup old fashioned oats
- ½ cup water
- ½ cup unsweetened almond milk
- 1 small ripe banana, sliced thin
- 1 Tbsp. brown sugar
- ½ tsp. vanilla essence
- ½ cup cherries, pitted then sliced in half
- 2 Tbsps. sliced almonds

Method:

- Combine oats, water, milk, and banana slices into a saucepan over medium heat.
- Once the mixture starts to bubble, stir continuously for about three minutes and use a spatula to mash in the banana slices. Remove pan from heat and stir in the small serving of brown sugar (optional), and vanilla essence. You can use almond extract here too.
- Top porridge with cherries and almonds.

Apple Pie and Dates Oatmeal:

Dates are the ultimate replacement for brown sugar when it comes to oatmeal. Actually, dates have taken the fitness world by storm in recent years and have been used as sugar alternatives as well as a vegan-friendly baking companion in many recent recipes. Their sticky sweetness gives the same feel as caramel, without the calories. This recipe is from *Minimalist Baker* and is the perfect thing to serve for breakfast or as a healthy dessert.

Ingredients:

- 2 tart or sweet apples (peeled, cored and evenly sliced)
- 1 tsp. honey/maple syrup (optional)
- ¼ tsp. ground cinnamon
- 1 tsp. lemon juice
- 1 cup old-fashioned rolled oats
- 1 cup water
- 1 cup unsweetened almond milk
- 1 pinch salt
- 4 whole dates (finely chopped)

Method:

- Preheat the oven to 350 degrees F.
- Line a baking sheet with parchment paper and toss apples with lemon juice, cinnamon, and honey. Bake for 5 minutes, then roll over parchment paper and tuck it in so they're in a "pocket" to trap in moisture. Cook for 10-15 minutes more (20 minutes total) until soft. Set aside.
- In a small saucepan over high heat, add oats, pinch salt, water, and almond milk and stir. When it comes to a boil, reduce to low-medium heat and cook until thick and creamy. Add the chopped dates a few minutes after you reduce the heat so they can soften and sweeten the oats.

- Once thick, remove from stove top. Add a little almond milk if it's too thick for your liking.
- Arrange ⅓ cup baked apples in the bottom of a serving bowl and top with oats. Other toppings may include nuts, nut butter, flaxseed, honey, maple syrup, or cinnamon. I prefer mine with a few toasted pecans and flaxseed. (Shlutz, October 2020)

Peanut Butter Cup Overnight Oats:

This vegan recipe can be served as breakfast or dessert and is deliciously low in calories. At just 274 calories per serving, this dish offers 10 grams of protein along with 9 grams of fiber. A breakfast that is well-balanced in fiber and protein will help avoid any sugar crashes from sugarier breakfasts, as well as promoting positive digestion. Protein will keep you fuller for longer. These peanut butter overnight oats will give you that sweet craving you are desiring without the consequences.

Peanut Butter Layer:

- 1 cup quick cooking oats
- 1 ¼ cups unsweetened almond milk
- 2 tsps. chia seeds
- 1 Tbsp. honey (maple syrup can work here too)
- 2 tsps. ground flax seed
- 2 Tbsps. all-natural peanut butter
- pinch of salt

Chocolate Layer:

- 1 cup quick cooking oats
- 1 ½ cups unsweetened almond milk
- 2 tsps. chia seeds
- 1 Tbsp. maple syrup
- 2 tsps. ground flax seed
- 3 Tbsps. cacao powder
- pinch of salt

Optional toppings:

- all natural peanut butter
- chocolate chips (go for cacao chocolate chips, with at least 85% cacao content)

Method:

For the Peanut Butter Layer:

- Place all ingredients into a glass tupperware and mix. Place in the refrigerator for at least 2 hours or overnight.
- For the Chocolate Layer:
- Place all ingredients into a glass tupperware and mix. Place in the refrigerator for at least 2 hours or overnight.
- For the Peanut Butter Cup Overnight Oats:
- In a jar (we used a ⅕ liter Weck jar), layer the peanut butter and chocolate overnight oat mixture. Top with all natural peanut butter and a few chocolate chips. (Funke, April 2021)

Pumpkin Spice Latte Overnight Oats:

For anyone who is one of the first in line during the fall when Starbucks starts selling their pumpkin spice lattes again, it might break your heart a little to look at the ingredients. 16 fl oz of this famous latte holds a whopping 380 calories, with 120 of those calories belonging to fat! Even more shocking than this is the 50 grams of sugar found in every grande latte! This is one of my favorite additions to fall and while I am sure I'm breaking your heart right now, don't close the book and give up on dieting just yet! Of course, treats can be enjoyed in moderation. Especially at my age, I have no interest in restricting myself. But I used to order one of these sugary lattes every day before work. This may explain the serious sugar crash that would come thereafter. Thankfully, lifestyle and recipe blogger Davida Lederle has come up with a healthy alternative. She even adds an espresso to this oat mixture that gives it a real pumpkin spice taste! Here, she has also included how to make your own pumpkin spice, which can be used for other recipes during autumn.

Ingredients:

- 1 cup rolled oats (not quick-cooking)
- ½ cup brewed coffee (or 2 espresso shots)
- ½ cup unsweetened almond milk or coconut milk
- ½ cup pumpkin puree
- 2 Tbsp. maple syrup
- 1 tsp. pumpkin spice
- 2 tsps. chia seeds

Method:

- Combine all ingredients in a jar or sealed container and give it a good shake.
- Place in the refrigerator overnight or for at least 6 hours.

- Heat up in the microwave if desired, or eat cold. (Lederle, Sept 2020)

Homemade Pumpkin Spice:

Ingredients:

- 3 Tbsp. ground cinnamon
- 1 ½ tsps. ground ginger
- 1 ½ tsps. ground nutmeg
- ¾ tsp. allspice
- ½ tsp. ground cloves
- For 1 tsp. of pumpkin spice:
- ½ tsp. ground cinnamon
- ¼ tsp. ground ginger
- ¼ tsp. ground nutmeg
- pinch of allspice
- pinch of cloves

Method:

- Add all ingredients to a bowl and stir.
- Store in a sealed spice jar to keep fresh. (Lederle, Sept 2020)

Healthy Breakfast Smoothies:

Have you ever wondered why your smoothies have prevented you from losing weight? How can having fruit for breakfast, with all of that added, more absorbable fiber, negatively impact weight loss?! The truth is, many store-bought smoothies are packed with sugars and too much of the sugary fruits and not enough vegetables, leafy greens, or protein. Fruit is wonderful for us, especially as a start to the day type-meal, since our body breaks it down quickly and it helps our digestive system to get going. But if you consume fruit-heavy smoothies that don't have ingredients to help balance out the sugars properly, then you will be absorbing high sugar and will more than likely crash an hour afterwards. Sugar crashes from fruity breakfasts can actually aid feelings of anxiety, since the quick dip in our blood sugar levels leaves us feeling strange. I am going to give you some of my best smoothie recipes, ones that actually work in promoting weight loss, beating bloat and other digestive issues, and serve as a perfect start to your day. If you want to alter any of these recipes, just bear in mind these key points to making the perfect healthy smoothie:

Fruit: Most of us are used to seeing pretty, pink smoothies decorated with pretty garnishes such as coconut shavings and seeds, or at least that's what Pinterest brings up. But more often than not, your smoothies will not be turning out this color! In fact, since I always like to add leafy greens to whatever smoothie I make, the color is usually more of a gloopy green! But don't let that turn you off. Fruit is an essential part of fiber, and good carbs that give us essential nutrients and fuel. Bananas for example will pack a potassium punch into your morning, so I always go with them. But be more mindful of the amount of fruit you are putting into your smoothie. Believe it or not, a ¼ of an apple and a couple of strawberries is enough to give you a sweet taste. Plus, the way I have written these recipes, the proteins such as the peanut butter or natural yogurt will balance out the taste and make it more well-rounded. So, if you have been packing your smoothies with four or five different fruits in one batch, stop now! It would be better to make a variety of smoothies throughout the week, using one of the five different fruits per day.

Natural/Kefir yogurt: If you have been avoiding adding natural yogurt to your smoothies for fear of calories or fat, then you are wrongly mistaken. Ironically, the healthy fats that can be found in natural yogurt and kefir milk have actually been proven to help reduce belly fat. More than that, natural yogurt and kefir contain some of the best friendly bacteria for your gut and digestive system to function properly. We often hear that our gut is our second brain, hence the phrase "trust your gut", but almost half the population are suffering from gut issues with an imbalance in bad bacteria. This is caused by antibiotic usage, poor diet, or excessive sugars and starch. But don't worry, there are ways that you can maintain it and produce healthy gut bacteria which will in turn reduce symptoms such as bloating, IBS, and constipation. The protein in natural yogurt is great for balancing out the sugars found in the fruit and milk. The creamy texture of yogurt is a great companion for smoothies. 1-2 tablespoons is usually enough.

Supplements: To me, breakfast smoothies are all about supplements. For those powder superfoods that you enjoy taking, smoothies are the best contenders to get them into you without much stress. I will never drink a smoothie without some kind of supplement. Especially for women our age, there are so many natural supplements that have a vast amount of benefits to our health. I cover supplements and their benefits to intermittent fasting and health in my book *The Complete and Simple Guide to Intermittent Fasting*, so take a look at it if you want an extensive look at supplement advantages and history. I have added a tablespoon of at least one supplement per recipe here. Of course, you don't have to add these powders to your smoothie, but nowadays, things like maca powder, wheatgrass, collagen, spirulina, and chlorella can be found in your local grocery store at affordable prices. So I would strongly recommend you do! As I mention in my other book, you want to look out for supplements that are not overly priced but where their origins are 100% traceable. For example, maca powder is Peruvian ginseng, and it should be sourced from the mountains in Peru. Look out for organic supplements and you should be just fine!

Water: This is such a simple step and it is so often forgotten. Have you ever made a smoothie and it has come out gloopy and chunky? Not ideal. This can be solved simply by adding a bit of water to your blender and blending the smoothie again for another 30-60 seconds. This is separate from the yogurt and milk. Water should be added towards the end to give the smoothie its finished smooth consistency. Also, bear in mind that it is better to use mineral water of good quality.

Nut Butter: Ever since I have put nut butter into my smoothies, I have noticed a massive difference in their ability to keep me slim as well as allowing me to stomach some of those more vegetable-centred juices. I usually use good quality peanut butter, one that contains no palm oil. In fact, a good quality peanut butter should only have one ingredient: peanuts! You can use cashew butter, coconut oil for keto eaters, or almond butter. Choose whichever one you naturally keep in the house and you will no longer be hoarding forgotten jars of peanut butter for years in a dusty cabinet.

Vegetables: There are ways of adding leafy greens and vegetables to your smoothies without having them overpower the taste. In fact, when you make smaller serving smoothies, you can add less ingredients, so that the taste is not overwhelming. I use about half a carrot per smoothie and mixed in with nut butter and strawberries, I really cannot trace the carrot flavor at all. Some more intense accompanying greens to smoothies include kale and spinach leaves. Kale is so rich in fiber that it benefits from being broken down and blended, but I prefer to use frozen spinach instead. A stalk of celery and a half a cucumber are also great veggies to pop into a smoothie without being overpowering.

Seeds: Raw chia seeds can be added into smoothies at the same time as the other ingredients and do not need to be absorbed overnight. In fact, adding them raw and then blending them will help make their fiber more absorbable. Flaxseeds added to smoothies will give you a necessary dose of omega-3 and omega-6 fatty acids. They blend very well in smoothies and give a slightly nuttier taste which I enjoy. Pumpkin seeds and sunflower seeds are excellent for topping and mixing into your smoothies. They also look pretty when serving up!

Remember these key points when wanting to adjust any of the smoothie recipes in this book, or when you want to make one off the cuff. Smoothies can also be meal-prepped and stored in an airtight jar in the freezer. Or an easier way of making morning smoothies is freezing chopped-up fruit as you buy it. I usually buy strawberries and bananas from my local greengrocer that don't have the longest shelf life, but are still juicy and full of flavor. I simply chop them up and pop them into tupperware for safekeeping. You can do the same with leafy greens and veggies too! That way, your smoothies are costing you next to nothing, since you may not have otherwise gotten around to eating the last of the fruits and veggies in your fridge.

Without further ado, let's take a look at some of my belly-busting all-time favorite smoothie recipes.

Gut-Healing Aloe Smoothie:

Aloe vera juice in a smoothie? Yes! Aloe has some remarkable properties that help heal the gut and promote digestive wellness. The taste is discreet enough that you won't be put off, but it certainly gives an interesting bite to it. This is more of a health juice than a smoothie, but it is an ideal way to get your metabolism going in the mornings. The lemon and ginger will compliment the aloe vera and hide the taste. This recipe is for those who experience gut problems, digestive issues, or feel bloated and tired when they wake up in the morning. I would strongly recommend you try this smoothie and reap the benefits!

Ingredients:

- 1 cup aloe vera juice. (You can slice into the flesh of an aloe stalk for extra freshness or buy the aloe juice in a store.)
- 1 ½ 2cup water, filtered
- ½ cucumber
- 1 whole lemon
- 1 Tbsp. minced ginger root
- 2 cups baby spinach
- 1 pinch sea salt
- 4 ice cubes
- pinch of cinnamon

Method:

- If you are using fresh aloe, snap or prune one thick stalk of aloe. Slice out the flesh by cutting the aloe leaf off and getting into the white flesh of the aloe plant.
- Put the aloe juice into a blender with the water, cucumber, lemon, ginger, baby spinach, cinnamon, water, sea salt, and ice cubes.
- Blend until smooth. Serve cold.

Aloe Strawberry Smoothie:

Talk about tropical! This beautiful smoothie is inspired by Andalusia in Spain, where I currently live. Here, plenty of aloe vera plants grow easily in the tropical climate. It is some of the best quality aloe you can find and many businesses source their aloe from this region. Strawberries are also grown in Spain and generally harvested during the Summer solstice. In fact, on the 25th June, there is a full moon that is nicknamed the "Strawberry moon". Native Americans believed that it was a sign for them to harvest their strawberries, and they were right. So, if you fancy getting a tropical taste of Spanish culture, then whip up this healthy, fat-burning smoothie.

- 1 cup pineapple, cubed
- 1 banana, peeled and sliced
- 4 slices of grapefruit, peeled
- 1 cup strawberries, washed
- 1 Tbsp. ginger, chopped
- 1 stalk of aloe vera or 4 Tbsp. of aloe vera juice
- ¾ cup filtered water
- ¾ cup almond milk
- 1 Tbsp. honey
- ¼ tsp. ground cinnamon
- 3 ice cubes

Method:

- If you are using fresh aloe, snap or prune one thick stalk of aloe. Slice out the flesh by cutting the aloe leaf off and getting into the white flesh of the aloe plant.
- Put the pineapple, banana, grapefruit, strawberries, ginger, aloe vera flesh, almond milk, honey, cinnamon, and ice cubes into a blender and blend.
- Add the water and blend once more before serving cold.

Gorgeous Green Smoothie:

This is the ultimate vegetable-packed smoothie. The lemon juice and green apple will allow you to absorb those leafy greens first thing in the morning without being overwhelmed by the veggie taste. The natural yogurt will further aid the sweet taste. All in all, this is a nutrient-dense, energy-packed, low-calorie, and low-sugar smoothie that has remarkable health benefits the more you turn to it in the mornings! The rich fiber will also leave you satisfied till about noon, but if it has awakened your digestive system, then feel free to have a boiled egg around 2 hours after consuming.

Ingredients:

- 1 cup spinach leaves
- ½ cup romaine lettuce leaves
- ½ cucumber, sliced 1 celery stalk, chopped
- ½ apple, sliced
- 1 tsp. spirulina powder
- ½ cup water, filtered juice of ½ lemon
- 1 Tbsp. natural peanut butter
- 2 Tbsp. natural yogurt

Method:

- Chop up the romaine lettuce, spinach leaves, cucumber, celery, and apple into small pieces and toss into the blender with ½ lemon juice.
- Add some mineral water and blend until mixture is still lumpy but mostly blended.
- Add in the peanut butter, yogurt, and spirulina powder.
- Blend again and add some more mineral water, if needed.
- When you have reached your desired consistency, serve.

Immune Booster Turmeric and Pineapple Smoothie:

You know that time of year where everyone tends to get the sniffles, and no matter how hard you try, at least one member of the family ends up sick in bed, passing it on to the rest of us? Well, in those colder months, when we are more prone to getting sick, this turmeric pineapple smoothie is an absolute must. Turmeric is a scientific superfood, and it is one of the most researched vegetables in the world, with over 14,000 studies associated with it! In Chinese and Indian traditional medicine, turmeric was used medicinally to treat joint pain and menstrual problems. It has also been known to reduce inflammation and can even reduce certain menopausal symptoms. This will clean out your liver and belly, so it is great to have after a night of heavy drinking of rich food consumption. So whether you are trying to fight against cold weather, build up your immune system for an important week, or relieve joint pain, this smoothie will give you everything you need and more.

Ingredients:

- 2 cups water
- 1 lemon, squeezed
- ½ tsp. ground turmeric
- ¼ tsp. ground ginger
- ⅛ tsp. cinnamon
- 1 Tbsp. honey

Serves 2, Store in the refrigerator in an airtight container.

Method:

- Mix together, water, lemon juice, turmeric, ginger, and cinnamon. Add honey, maple syrup, or vanilla essence to taste. Add 1-2 ice cubes to chill. Serve cold.

Glowing Skin Smoothie:

This smoothie has collagen added to the recipe which will aid to a better complexion, as well as the reduction of fine lines and wrinkles. Collagen is also best known for strengthening bones, and can also improve your skin's elasticity. Collagen supplements are hot on the market now, and there are some that are completely overpriced, in my opinion. Collagen is produced naturally by the body, but this deteriorates as we get older. Collagen in supplement form has been around for decades and you should be able to get a high-quality, cost-effective supplement without having to break the bank. Add 1 scoop to each smoothie and try to find one that contains magnesium and hyaluronic acid in it also.

Ingredients:

- 2 cups kale or
- 2 cups baby spinach
- 1 cup green apple
- ½ cucumber
- 1 lemon squeezed
- 1 banana
- ice
- 1 tsp. fresh ginger grated
- 1 scoop serving collagen powder
- 1 scoop serving vitamin c powder (optional)

Method:

- Combine all ingredients together, adding water where necessary, and serve cold.

Tropical Mango Booster Smoothie:

This smoothie is on the sweeter side, in order to balance out the strong taste of turmeric that some people find difficult to stomach. But please, not let this stop you from putting turmeric in your smoothies, the health benefits are just too great. The mango flavors in this smoothie give it a classical India-inspired taste, and they pair together beautifully. The peaches will further help balance out the turmeric and the additional natural yogurt gives this a creamy delicious texture. Great for inflammation, improved skin, improved digestion, and weight loss.

Ingredients:

- 1 cup peaches
- 1 cup mangoes
- 1 cup almond milk, unsweetened
- 1 Tbsp. natural yogurt
- 1 tsp. turmeric
- ¼ tsp. ginger
- 1 scoop collagen powder

Method:

- Combine all ingredients together until well combined and smooth. Add a teaspoon of honey for taste, if desired. Serve chilled by freezing the mango and pineapple, or by adding 1-2 ice cubes made from mineral water.

Cacao Blueberry Smoothie:

I try to add at least a tsp. of cacao into every smoothie I make. The taste gives me the familiar reminiscence of a chocolate milkshake, and the health benefits are incomparable! Cacao powder is made from cacao, just like cocoa powder. The difference is that cocoa powder beans are roasted to make the creamy chocolate that we all know and recognize. Cacao powder on the other hand is not as intensely roasted and, for that reason, stays pure and retains its nutrients. 100% natural cacao powder is easy to find and inexpensive. In every case, when you used to use cocoa powder, use cacao powder instead. Not only is it a superfood but it also has a rich, delicious taste.

Ingredients:

- 1 cup almond milk
- 1 scoop cacao powder
- ½ cup blueberries
- 1 cup spinach
- 1 banana
- 1 Tbsp. cashew butter, peanut butter, or almond butter
- ice

Method:

- Blend together the almond milk, cacao powder, blueberries, spinach, banana, and cashew butter or nut butter of your choice. Add with ice if desired.

Apple and Spinach Kiwi Smoothie:

Ingredients:

- 1 banana, peeled
- 1 large green apple, cored and chopped (keep the skins for extra fiber)
- 3 kiwis, peeled and cubed
- 1 cup natural yogurt
- 1 cup water
- 2 cups spinach

Method:

- Blend together all ingredients, adding more or less water as needed. Serve cold by adding 1-2 ice cubes.

Basic Breakfast Smoothie:

This protein-packed breakfast smoothie is perfect for getting your digestive system going gently and in a balanced way. The fiber from the fruit and veggies is easier to digest since it has been blended, the Spirulina packs 4 out of its 7 grams of protein into the mix. The Tbsp. of peanut butter will help balance the sugars from the fruit and the flaxseeds will give some omega-3 for your brain to function to the best of its ability.

Ingredients:

- 1 bunch of spinach leaves (frozen or fresh)
- 3 medium-sized strawberries
- 1 celery stick, chopped up
- cucumber slices (4 to 6 slices, or whatever you prefer)
- 3 grams of blueberries
- half an apple
- 1 Tbsp. of spirulina
- 4 Tbsps. of almond milk
- 2 Tbsps. of flaxseed
- mixed seeds to garnish
- 3 Tbsps. of kefir natural yogurt

Method:

- Place all of the ingredients into a smoothie blender. You may use a hand blender also, but make sure that your vegetables and fruit are chopped up small enough for it to blend.
- Blend all ingredients together until it is liquid-based and there are no lumps.
- Enjoy in a tall glass and garnish with some mixed seeds.

Other Breakfast Favorites:

Poached Egg and Smashed Avocado on Toast

This is a delicious, filling breakfast that is full of healthy fats and protein. Avocados are a great source of monounsaturated fats, potassium, and fiber, while eggs have micronutrients such as Vitamins B and D, as well as protein. I have suggested sourdough bread as the base, but you can choose any sprouted whole grain bread to serve on. Serve with a cup of black coffee for added taste and full retention.

Ingredients:

- 1 small, ripe avocado
- 3 cherry tomatoes cut in half
- 1 medium-sized egg
- 1 tsp. of lime
- 1 slice of sourdough bread
- kosher salt and freshly ground pepper

Method:

- Halve and stone the avocado, and place the flesh into a small bowl.
- Mash the avocado with a fork and add the squeeze of lime juice, with some salt and pepper.
- Heat a pan of water, gently break in the egg, and leave to poach for 1 to 2 minutes until the whites have firmed but the yolks are runny.
- Alternatively, you can poach your egg by lining a cup with a cling film cover. Form a semi-circle around the cup with the cling film, so that the egg can be dropped into the film and then sealed. The cling film will allow the egg to keep its poached shape and can be removed easily when the egg has been poached.

- When the poached egg has formed, take it out of the pot of boiling water and set down on a chopping board, if cling film needs to be removed, and gently remove it. The egg should be hard enough that it will retain its shape.
- Toast the slice of sourdough bread and add the mashed avocado, chopped tomatoes, and poached egg.
- Garnish with kosher salt and black pepper

Low-Fat Feta Cheese Omelette

Omelets are incredibly filling and versatile. You can add or remove any of these ingredients, other than the eggs and feta. Feta is already lower in fat than a lot of other cheeses, but it should still be eaten in moderation. Since it is not made from cow's milk, but from sheep and goats, it is actually easier for our bodies to digest. Anything that is in your fridge from leftovers—chicken, peppers, spinach, red onion—can be put into the mixture.

Ingredients:

- 2 medium-sized eggs
- a small portion of chopped mixed peppers
- 1 bunch of spinach
- 2 cloves of garlic, chopped up
- 4 to 6 cherry tomatoes, cut in half
- 1 tsp. of cilantro powder
- 4 to 6 small cubes of low-fat feta cheese
- kosher salt and pepper
- 1 bunch of cilantro to garnish

Method:

- Crack the 2 eggs into a bowl together with the spinach, garlic, tomatoes, feta cheese, cilantro, and peppers.
- Whisk all ingredients together. At the same time, heat a skillet over a medium temperature with a dollop of natural butter.
- When the butter has melted, pour the ingredients into the skillet and allow it to cook the bottom half of the omelet.
- After 5 minutes, flip the omelet over to the other side. Don't worry if it folds into itself. Allow the feta cheese cubes to melt within the mixture.
- Serve with some extra spinach leaves on the side and garnish with cilantro.

Healthy Overnight Oatmeal

Oatmeal is such a versatile breakfast. Allowing the oats to soak overnight gets rids of the starches and allows you to absorb the nutritional value of the meal better. This breakfast is perfect for an everyday go-to as well as those times in the year when it starts to get chilly.

The berries contain antioxidants, the water cuts out on the calories of milk, the cinnamon is an excellent alternative to sugar, which also provides anti-inflammatory properties, and the peanut butter is for protein. You can use peanut butter powder.

It is like a warm hug in the morning, and the fruit, oats, and flaxseed pack it with vitamins and nutrients. The chia seeds are excellent for digestion and also battle things such as bloating. This breakfast is filling, simple, and cost-effective.

Ingredients:

- 1 cup of oats
- 1 cup of plant-based milk
- 1 Tbsp. of chia seeds
- 1 Tbsp. of flaxseed
- 1 tsp. of cacao powder
- 1 Tbsp. of peanut butter (optional)
- a small handful of raspberries and blueberries
- 1 tsp. of cinnamon

Method:

- Soak the oats, cacao powder, and chia seeds in distilled water overnight. This will get rid of some of the starches in the oats and will make them easier to digest and absorb.
- Drain the water out of the oat mixture and place it into a saucepan.

- Add in 1 cup of plant-based milk to the oat mixture, more if needed, and put on low-medium heat, while stirring with a wooden spoon and mixing in a teaspoon of cinnamon.
- Pour the mixture into a bowl and stir in the tablespoons of peanut butter.
- Place the berries on top of the oatmeal mixture for serving, and enjoy.

Lunch Recipes

Summer Allotment Salad with English Mustard Dressing:

Ingredients:

- 400g new-season potatoes, scrubbed
- 2 bunches of radishes, leaves washed
- 1 red onion, peeled and sliced
- 1 small cucumber, peeled, deseeded and sliced into half moons
- small handful dill fronds, chopped

For the dressing:

- 100ml rapeseed oil
- 20g english mustard
- 1 Tbsp. white wine vinegar
- pinch of white caster sugar
- 1 Tbsp. mustard seeds, toasted in a dry frying pan

Method:

- Bring a pan of salted water to boil, simmer the potatoes for about 10 mins until tender, then leave to steam-dry until warm.
- Meanwhile, whisk together all the dressing ingredients, then halve the warm potatoes and toss through the dressing. Take the potatoes and other ingredients to the picnic separately, then toss everything together to serve. (Kerridge, August 2018)

Charred Corn, Chicken & Tortilla Salad with Chipotle Yogurt Dressing:

Ingredients:

- 1 Tbsp. smoked paprika, plus ½ tsp.
- 1 tsp. dried oregano
- 1 Tbsp. chipotle paste, plus 1 tsp.
- ½ tsp. cinnamon
- 2 garlic cloves, crushed
- 2 limes, 1 zested and juiced, 1 cut into wedges to serve
- 3 Tbsp. olive oil, plus extra for brushing and frying
- 6 boneless, skinless chicken thighs
- 150g natural yogurt
- 2 tsps. honey
- 2 corns on the cob, husks removed if needed
- 2 little Gem lettuces, halved through the core, leaves pulled apart and torn
- 400g can black beans, drained, rinsed and drained again
- 200g cherry tomatoes, halved
- 2 avocados, stoned, peeled, halved and cut into chunks
- 2 corn tortilla wraps
- small bunch of coriander, leaves picked and roughly chopped

Method:

- Mix 1 Tbsp. paprika, the oregano, 1 Tbsp. chipotle, cinnamon, garlic, lime zest and 2 Tbsps. oil together in a bowl with some seasoning. Pour over the chicken thighs, turning to coat, then cover and chill for at least a few hours, or up to 24 hrs.
- Light the barbecue and let the flames die down, or heat a griddle pan over a high heat. Mix the yogurt, lime juice, the remaining oil, ½ tsp. paprika, 1 tsp.

chipotle and honey with a pinch of salt. Set aside. Brush the corn cobs with a little oil, then cook it and the marinated chicken on the barbecue or in the griddle pan for about 10 mins, turning often until the chicken is cooked through (it should be charred and firm to the touch—check it's done by cutting into one of the thickest pieces) and the corn is bright yellow and juicy.
- Transfer the chicken and corn to a board or plate and cover to keep warm. Arrange the lettuce, beans, tomatoes, and avocado on a large platter or in a serving bowl, but wait to toss together until just before serving—this helps keep the lettuce leaves from wilting.
- Cut the wraps into strips or small pieces. Heat a drizzle of oil in a frying pan and fry the strips until crisp and golden, then drain on kitchen paper. Sprinkle it with salt.
- Slice the cooked chicken into 1cm strips and cut the charred corn from the cob. Add to the salad, then drizzle over the dressing and any juice from the chicken and toss. Scatter over the coriander and crispy tortilla strips, and serve with the lime wedges on the side. (Best, June 2020)

Roasted Beetroot & Raw Honey Salad:

Ingredients:

- 3 large beetroot, cut into wedges
- 2 Tbsp. rapeseed oil
- 5 thyme sprigs
- 25g feta, crumbled
- 1 Tbsp. honey
- 200g canned green lentils, drained
- 50g rocket
- 30g mixed seeds
- small handful of dill, to serve

Method:

- Heat the oven to 390 degrees F. Toss the beetroot, ½ Tbsp. oil and the thyme in a roasting tin. Season. Roast for 30-35 mins or until tender, adding the feta for the last 10 mins. Leave to cool slightly.
- Whisk the remaining oil with the honey, a splash of cold water to loosen and some seasoning. Warm the lentils in a pan or microwave, then season. Toss the beetroot and feta with the rocket and dressing, then serve on top of the lentils with the seeds and dill scattered over. (Clark, Aug 2020)

Quinoa, Goat's Cheese & Peach Salad:

Ingredients:

- 200g quinoa
- 100g chard, finely shredded
- 4 peaches or nectarines, stoned, 2 quartered and 2 finely sliced
- 1-2 lemons, juiced
- 4-5 Tbsp. extra virgin olive oil
- 50g hazelnuts, roughly chopped
- 25g parsley, leaves picked and finely chopped
- 25g mint, leaves picked and finely chopped, plus extra mint leaves to serve
- 4 Tbsp. capers, drained
- 2 Tbsp. sumac (optional)
- 1-2 Tbsp. red wine vinegar
- 100g soft goat's cheese, crumbled
- 2-3 Tbsp. sesame seeds, toasted

Method:

- Heat the oven to 390 degrees F and cook the quinoa following pack instructions. Drain, mix with the chard, then set aside to cool and wilt.
- Put the sliced peaches in a bowl, drizzle over the lemon juice, and set aside. Put the quartered peaches on a baking tray. Toss with 1 Tbsp. olive oil. Roast for 10-15 mins until soft. Scatter the hazelnuts over a second baking tray and toast in the oven for the last 5 mins until golden.
- Combine the quinoa mix, herbs, sliced peaches, the capers, sumac (if using), vinegar, and remaining oil. Season. Put on a large serving plate, and top with the roasted peaches, goat's cheese, hazelnuts, sesame seeds and extra mint leaves. (McLuskie, July 2020)

Green Goddess Chicken Salad:

Ingredients:

- 1 large avocado, stoned, peeled and chopped
- ½ Tbsp. olive oil
- 1 lime, zested and juiced
- ½ jalapeño, deseeded
- ½ small bunch of basil, torn
- ½ cucumber, sliced diagonally
- 2 medium eggs
- 3 little gem lettuces, quartered
- 50g sundried tomatoes
- 2 cooked skinless chicken breasts, shredded
- 2 spring onions, shredded
- 200g cooked quinoa
- 1 Tbsp. chopped pistachios

Method:

- Put the avocado, oil, lime zest and juice, jalapeño, basil, half the cucumber and 1 Tbsp. water in a blender and blitz until smooth. Season to taste, then set aside in the fridge until ready to use.
- Cook the eggs in a pan of boiling water for 7 mins, then rinse under cold running water to cool. Drain, peel, and halve, then set aside.
- Toss the lettuce quarters with the sun dried tomatoes, cooked chicken, the spring onions and remaining cucumber. Spread the cooked quinoa over the base of a serving plate, then top with the chicken salad, eggs, and the dressing. Scatter over the pistachios and serve. (Clark, June 2020)

Herby Orzo & Lemon Salad:

Ingredients:

- 1 Tbsp. olive oil
- 1 Tbsp. butter
- 1 red onion, finely chopped
- 1 garlic clove, finely grated
- ½ Tbsp. light brown soft sugar
- 350g orzo
- 50ml extra virgin olive oil
- 1 large lemon, juiced
- 1 small bunch of basil, finely chopped
- 1 small bunch parsley, finely chopped
- 2 Tbsp. capers, drained and rinsed
- 50g flaked almonds, lightly toasted

Method:

- Heat the olive oil and butter in a non-stick frying pan over a medium heat, and fry the onion for 10-15 mins, or until golden and caramelized. Add the garlic and sugar and cook for a further 3 mins. Season to taste.
- Cook the orzo following pack instructions. Drain, then toss with a little of the extra virgin olive oil and leave to cool completely. Whisk the remaining oil with the lemon juice and set aside.
- Toss the orzo with the sticky onion and garlic, the lemony dressing, herbs, capers, and half the toasted almonds. Season. Spoon onto a sharing plate and top with the rest of the almonds. Will keep in the fridge for up to three days. (Clark, Aug 2020)

Tomato & Mozzarella Salad with Tomato Dressing:

Ingredients:

- 200g mixed heritage tomatoes, sliced
- 1 large shallot, sliced into thin rings
- 5 Tbsp. olive oil
- 3 drops of Tabasco sauce
- 1 Tbsp. white wine vinegar
- 6 basil leaves, shredded, plus extra small leaves to serve
- 4 shop-bought crostini, roughly crushed
- 1 ball buffalo mozzarella, or burrata if you can find it (about 150g), halved

Method:

- Put the tomatoes in a bowl with the shallots and season with a large pinch of salt. Leave for 10 mins for the tomatoes to release their juices.
- Lift the tomatoes and shallots out of the bowl using a slotted spoon, and reserve the juices. Arrange the tomatoes over two plates, then sprinkle over the shallots.
- Whisk the olive oil, Tabasco and vinegar into the reserved tomato juices to make a dressing. Drizzle over the tomatoes and shallots, then scatter with the shredded basil and crushed crostini. Put one half of the mozzarella in the centre of each plate, and season with freshly ground black pepper. Top with the extra basil leaves, and serve. (Kerridge, July 2020)

Peach & Raspberry Fruit Salad with Mascarpone:

Ingredients:

- 2 ripe peaches or nectarines
- 50g caster sugar
- 1 tsp. lemon thyme leaves
- 100g mascarpone
- 100ml double cream
- drop vanilla extract
- 16 raspberries, halved
- small handful pistachios, roughly chopped
- 1 Tbsp. maple syrup

Method:

- Stone and finely slice the peaches or nectarines and arrange the slices over four plates. Sprinkle over a little of the sugar and scatter over most of the thyme leaves.
- Whisk together the mascarpone, cream, vanilla extract and the remaining sugar in a bowl until light and fluffy. Spoon or pipe blobs of the mixture over the peaches or nectarines and arrange the raspberries over the plates. Finish with a scattering of pistachios, the remaining thyme leaves and a drizzle of maple syrup to serve. (Kerridge, June 2019)

Cauliflower Steaks with Roasted Red Pepper & Olive Salsa:

Ingredients:

- 1 cauliflower
- ½ tsp. smoked paprika
- 2 Tbsp. olive oil
- 1 roasted red pepper
- 4 black olives, pitted
- small handful parsley
- 1 tsp. capers
- ½ Tbsp. red wine vinegar
- 2 Tbsp. toasted flaked almonds

Method:

- Heat oven to 390 degrees F and line a baking tray with parchment paper. Slice the cauliflower into two 1-inch steaks—use the middle part as it's larger, and save the rest for another time. Rub the paprika and ½ Tbsp. oil over the steaks and season. Put on the tray and roast for 15-20 mins until cooked through.
- Meanwhile, make the salsa. Chop the pepper, olives, parsley, and capers, and put into a bowl and mix with the remaining oil and vinegar. Season to taste. When the steaks are cooked, spoon over the salsa and top with flaked almonds to serve. (Godwin, July 2018)

Best Ever Potato Salad:

Ingredients:

- 800g baby potatoes
- 2 tsps. wholegrain mustard
- 2 Tbsp. muscatel or white wine vinegar
- 4 Tbsp. olive oil
- 1 shallot, very finely chopped
- 3 Tbsp. mayonnaise
- 2 Tbsp. sour cream
- 1 Tbsp. horseradish sauce
- ¼ lemon, juiced
- 2 spring onions, finely sliced
- handful of crispy fried onions

Method:

- Tip the potatoes into a large pan of cold salted water. Bring to boil, then simmer for 10 mins until tender to the tip of a knife.
- While the potatoes are cooking, whisk the mustard, vinegar, olive oil, and chopped shallot together with a good pinch of salt and a grind of pepper. When the potatoes are cool enough to handle, peel if you prefer, then halve, quarter or cut them into bite-sized chunks if large, then toss in the mustard dressing until completely coated. Leave to cool completely.
- Meanwhile, mix the mayonnaise, sour cream, lemon juice, and horseradish together. When the potatoes are cool, toss them through the mayonnaise mixture along with the spring onions. Tip into a dish and scatter with the crispy onions just before serving, or serve the crispy onions on the side for sprinkling over at the table. (Desmazery, June 2020)

Roasted Asparagus and Pea Salad:

Ingredients:

- 3 Tbsp. natural yogurt
- 1 tsp. wholegrain mustard
- ½ tsp. honey
- ½ lemon, zested and juiced
- 100g watercress
- 1 large slice sourdough bread
- 200g asparagus, tough ends removed
- 1 ½ Tbsp. cold-pressed rapeseed oil
- 2 eggs
- 200g frozen peas

Method:

- Heat oven to 390 degrees F. Mix the yogurt, mustard, and honey together. Add the lemon zest, then add the juice and some seasoning to taste. Squeeze any remaining lemon juice over the watercress.
- Tear the bread into large pieces and put them on a roasting tray with the asparagus. Toss both in the rapeseed oil and seasoning, and roast for 10 mins until the asparagus is tender and croutons are golden.
- Meanwhile, cook the eggs in a pan of boiling water for 6 mins, then add the frozen peas and cook for 1 min more. Drain and rinse both under cold water until cool. Peel the eggs, then cut into quarters.
- To assemble, mix the asparagus and peas through the watercress, then toss through the creamy dressing. Nestle in the eggs and croutons, and serve. (Godwin, July 2018)

Healthy Waldorf Chicken Salad

This is a delicious, easy, and healthy salad. It is so tasty that I imagine you will want to repeat this meal several times a week. The natural Kefir yogurt will feed your gut friendly bacteria and will aid in positive digestion. It also cuts out a lot of calories, added salts, and sugars from other salad dressings. The cheese, chicken, and walnuts contain filling proteins to curb off any cravings until dinnertime.

Ingredients:

- 1 small breast of grilled chicken
- iceberg lettuce (as much as you desire)
- 3 Tbsps. of Kefir Natural yogurt
- 1 stalk of celery, chopped up
- half a cucumber, chopped up
- ¼ cup of walnuts, chopped up
- ½ cup of low-fat cheddar cheese, chopped up into cubes
- ½ a green apple, chopped up
- mixed seeds (optional)

Method:

- Place the chicken breast in the grill and time it so that it has around 5 minutes left to cook while you are preparing the other ingredients.
- Chop up the celery, cucumber, walnuts, apple, and cheese.
- Shred some iceberg lettuce into a large salad bowl and add your chopped ingredients.
- Add the grilled chicken, cut into small pieces, and mix the Kefir natural yogurt into the bowl.
- Serve and enjoy! If you have leftovers, you can keep them in the fridge for 1 to 2 days.

Shaved Carrot and Radish Salad

This salad is inventive, light, colorful, and summery. It also gives you a nice break from lettuce, if you have been eating predominantly salads for lunch for a couple of days. The shaved carrots and thinly sliced radishes mix perfectly with the tart citrus and honey vinaigrette. Making your own vinaigrette cuts back on any hidden ingredients, and means that this salad is completely focused on whole foods and nutrition. Also, having the olive oil fresh in your salad means you get to absorb the healthy fats of the oil without the negative impacts that can happen when olive oil is cooked at a certain temperature.

Ingredients:

- 4 large carrots, shaved vertically (you may use a potato peeler for this)
- 4 radishes, shaved around
- 1 small beet, shaved into half circles
- 2 small oranges, sliced into half circles
- A small bunch of fresh mint leaves
- vinaigrette ingredients
- 3 Tbsps. of fresh orange juice
- 3 Tbsps. of fresh lemon juice
- 1 tsp. of honey
- 3 Tbsps. of olive oil
- kosher salt and freshly ground black pepper to garnish

Method:

- In a salad bowl, whisk together the honey, orange juice, lemon juice, and a pinch of salt and pepper.
- Once the ingredients have blended in with the honey, add the olive oil and whisk once more.
- Place the shaved vegetables, cut oranges, and the mint to garnish on a plate and drizzle the vinaigrette over.

Homemade Falafel

Falafel is incredibly versatile, and you can have a lot of fun with the type of ingredients you like to put it with. The mixture itself keeps for up to 4 days in the fridge, as do the falafels, so it is a perfect thing to meal prep, especially if you are more likely to eat plant-based. It is satisfying and enjoyable preparing your own falafel from scratch and you also have all of the control over what actually goes into it!

Ingredients:

- uncooked chickpeas (this mixture works especially well with uncooked dried chickpeas and you may soak them overnight before making the falafel)
- 1 tsp. of lemon juice
- 1 shallot, chopped up
- 2 cloves of garlic, chopped up
- 1 tsp. of cayenne pepper
- 1 tsp. of cumin
- 1 tsp. of coriander
- 1 pinch of baking powder, to help the balls rise
- 1 pinch of kosher salt
- 1 bunch of cilantro
- 1 bunch of parsley
- 1 Tbsp. of olive oil

Method:

- Blend all ingredients together, preferably in a food processor, since this will help the chickpeas to blend well, and pulse the mixture until it is blended well, but not overly so.
- Shape the falafel mixture into small, round balls, on a baking tray with some baking paper lining it. There should be about two Tbsps. of mixture per ball. (The more you make, the more you have to store for the week! This mixture should make up to 15 falafel balls)

- Drizzle the olive oil over the falafel balls and place them in the oven to bake for 10 to 15 minutes, turning them halfway through.
- Serve on some pitta bread with hummus, radish, and cherry tomatoes, and enjoy!

Moroccan-Style Chicken

Sticking with the Moroccan-style food, here is a delicious Moroccan-style chicken that can be added to salads, pittas, or healthy whole grain bread. The spices, apricot, and herbs give the chicken an exotic flavor, especially if you feel as if you have been having plain chicken for too long! The cashew nuts and natural yogurt garnish means that this is really an excellent, protein-packed dish, without the need for any other carbs.

Ingredients:

- 1 medium-sized chicken breast
- 2 tsps. of ground cinnamon
- 1 tsp. of ground ginger
- 2 tsps. of clear honey
- 1 bunch of fresh coriander, chopped
- 3 garlic cloves, crushed
- 1 apricot, destoned and sliced
- 1 handful of cashew nuts
- 1 Tbsp. of natural yogurt

Method:

- Spread the cashew nuts on tin foil on a baking tray and roast them lightly on the lowest setting of the grill for 10 minutes.
- Grate the fresh ginger into a bowl with the honey, salt, and coat the chicken with these ingredients.
- Bake the chicken in the oven until cooked on the outside.
- Add the garlic, chopped apricot, and cashew nuts and mix them together, cooking for 15 minutes on a low heat.
- Serve with natural yogurt, and enjoy!

Dinner Recipes

Easy Chicken Soup

Chicken and vegetable soup is incredibly easy to make and has enormous nutritional benefits, especially when you make your stock naturally, which is a lot easier to do than you may realize! It is also a great way of using up the last bit of chicken and aiding the benefits of collagen and gut-friendly benefits from the bone broth.

Some people swear by bone broth so much that they drink a cup of it every day. You can mix up the veggies to whatever you prefer. This is a great dish for those colder months, when you aren't too fussed about making dinner and would rather make a big bowl of something to use throughout the week. You can store and even freeze the leftovers to use again when you are ready to.

Ingredients:

- 1 chicken carcass, with all skin and smaller bones removed
- 3 medium-sized rooster potatoes, with the skin on, chopped into fours
- 3 medium-sized carrots, chopped up
- 2 stalks of celery, chopped up
- 1 leek, chopped up
- 1 white onion, chopped up

Method:

- First, you will need to prepare the chicken carcass and allow it to stay on the hob for at least 3 hours. Cover the carcass with water and a pinch of salt. Keep it on the stove for a number of hours and allow the water to evaporate slightly and form into a broth.

- Take the carcass out of the broth, you may want to do this by draining the broth into a separate soup pot, and throw out the carcass.
- Add the vegetables and cover with 3 cups of water, if necessary, ensuring that all of the vegetables are able to cook and be covered consistently.
- Bring the soup to a boil and allow it to simmer for as long as you like (the longer the soup has had to simmer, the tastier it tends to be).
- Blend the soup, partly, to leave some nice thick chunks of vegetables, and serve with parsley and a small Tbsp. of some natural yogurt.

Healthy Broccoli Cheese Soup:

I have tried broccoli soup without cheese and trust me, it's not that exciting. You don't have to be overly restricted when you are dieting. Part of the fun is finding inventive ways to make your old favorites, but with a healthier twist! It really is all about the ingredients you use. For this recipe, there is no heavy cream or flour, which cuts out a lot of unnecessary calories and fat. Instead, you can use just two Tbsps. of butter and 5 oz shredded cheese, which are small and considerate portions, helping this soup to come in at just 237 calories per serving!

Serves 8. Calories: 237 kcal.

Ingredients:

- 2 Tbsp. butter
- 3 garlic cloves minced
- 1 onion finely chopped
- 5 cups butternut squash cubed
- 3 cups 2 large potatoes, cubed
- 4 cups any stock low sodium
- 3 cups any milk I used unsweetened almond
- 5 cups 1 lb broccoli, coarsely chopped
- 1 ¼ tsps. salt
- 5 oz sharp cheese shredded (cheddar is good for this). You can use low-fat cheese if you prefer.

Method:

- Preheat a large heavy bottom pot or dutch oven on medium heat and melt butter. Add garlic and onion, cook for 5 minutes, stirring occasionally.
- Add butternut squash, potatoes, stock and milk; bring to a boil. Reduce heat to low-medium, cover and cook for 7 minutes.

- Add broccoli and salt, bring to a boil, cover and cook for 4 more minutes. Turn off heat.
- If you like chunky soup (I do), remove broccoli into a bowl with a slotted spoon. Using an immersion blender, puree soup until smooth and silky. Return broccoli and add 4 oz of cheese; stir until cheese has melted. Serve hot sprinkled with remaining cheese. (Osipov, Dec 2020)

Carrot and Coriander Soup:

Coming in at the lowest calorie soup on the menu, this carrot and coriander classic soup is just 102 calories per serving (so feel free to have more than one bowl!) This carrot and coriander soup recipe serves 4 people and will take around 35 mins to prepare and cook, so you won't even have to spend that long in the kitchen to prepare it. Leftovers can be stored in an airtight container in the fridge for up to 3 days.

Serves 4. Calories: 102 kcal

Ingredients:

- 1Tbsp. vegetable oil
- 1 onion, chopped
- 450g carrots, washed and sliced
- 1 clove garlic, crushed
- 1tsp. ground coriander
- 1.2 ltr vegetable stock
- 3 Tbsp. chopped fresh coriander
- squeeze of lemon juice
- freshly grated nutmeg to taste
- salt and freshly ground black pepper

Method:

- Sauté the onions, carrots, and garlic in a large pan with the oil for 4 mins. Once they have softened, but not colored, add the ground coriander and stir. Season with salt and black pepper.
- Pour the vegetable stock into the pan and bring to a boil. Cover the pan and simmer until the carrots are tender, this should take around 20 mins.
- Stir through the fresh coriander, remove from the heat and blend the soup, adding the lemon juice, nutmeg and seasoning to taste as you do. You can use

- a hand blender or a food processor to blend your soup.
- The soup will have cooled whilst blending, so if you plan to eat it right away, gently reheat the soup, without boiling it, and serve. If you are saving it for later, allow it to cool and place in an airtight container in the fridge or freezer. (Dady, August 2020)

Thai Chicken Noodle Soup:

This Thai chicken noodle soup is absolutely bursting with flavor. It contains those signature Thai aromas of lemongrass, coriander, shallots, ginger, and red curry paste. The coconut milk and lime juice even smells delicious when you are preparing the ingredients! It is an impressive-looking dish which requires little effort. Rotisserie chicken works really well here, but you can use boneless or breast of chicken, if you prefer.

Serves 3. Calories: 282 kcal.

Ingredients:

- 4 ½ lbs. boneless skinless chicken breast, cooked and shredded
- 3 Tbsp. coconut oil
- 3 cup red onion, thinly sliced
- 6 garlic cloves, minced
- 3 Tbsp. minced fresh ginger
- 9 Tbsp. red curry paste
- 18 cup chicken broth
- 6 carrots, sliced
- 1 ½ cup halved snow peas
- 3 red pepper, julienned
- 24 oz. brown rice noodles
- 42 oz. coconut milk (in a can)
- 6 Tbsps. of fresh lime juice
- 1 cup fresh cilantro diced

- optional: top with sliced avocado and sliced green onions

Method:

- Heat a large dutch oven or soup pot to medium-high heat.
- Add in coconut oil. Once melted add red onions, saute until translucent, about 3-4 minutes. Next add in the garlic and ginger. Saute for 30 seconds, until fragrant, stirring the entire time.
- Add in the red curry paste, stir the paste into the aromatics (onion, garlic, and ginger) until it thickens, about 2-3 minutes.
- Next, add in the chicken broth. Bring to a boil and reduce to a simmer. Add in the shredded chicken.
- In the meantime bring a medium pot filled with water to a boil. Add brown rice noodles to the pot and cook for 4 minutes. (or whatever your directions say) Remove from the pot, drain water, and cool the noodles with cold water to stop the cooking process.
- Add noodles, carrots, red pepper, and snow peas to the chicken broth pot.
- Scoop about a cup of the broth out of the pot and add it to a blender or food processor, along with a can of coconut milk. Blend until the mixture looks creamy and the broth and milk no longer separate.
- Add the coconut milk mixture back to the soup pot. Stir and simmer for 5 minutes.
- Right before you're about to serve it. Finish the soup with fresh lime juice and fresh cilantro. Stir and serve!
- Optional: top with sliced avocado and sliced green onions. (JoyfulHealthyEats, Aug 2017)

Tuscan Tomato Soup and Rosemary Garlic Croutons:

Let's take a look at JoyfulHealthyEat's version of a classic Tuscan tomato soup. There is nothing as nostalgic as a warm bowl of tomato soup, and certainly for me, I absolutely love the aromas that come with making a batch of this. The rosemary and basil pair perfectly together.

Serves 1. Calories: 236 kcal.

Ingredients:

- 1 Tbsps. of olive oil
- 1 large onion, diced
- 3 garlic cloves, minced
- 2 Tbsps. of tomato paste
- 2 lbs. of roma tomatoes, seeds removed, chopped
- 2 15 oz. cans of no-salt added white beans, drained & rinsed
- 1 quart low sodium vegetable broth
- 1 cup of water
- 1 sprig of fresh rosemary
- ½ tsp. red pepper flakes
- rosemary garlic croutons:
- 4 cups of ciabatta bread, cubed
- 2 Tbsps. of olive oil
- ½ cup of mozzarella cheese
- 2 garlic cloves, minced
- 1 Tbsp. of fresh rosemary, chopped
- 2 Tbsps. of fresh basil, chopped

Method:

- Preheat the oven to 400 degrees F.
- Heat a small pan to medium-low heat, add 2 Tbsps. of olive oil and 2 garlic cloves. Cook, stirring occasionally until garlic is lightly browned. {about 3-5 minutes}

- Spread ciabatta bread out of the baking sheet, pour garlic oil mixture on top, as well as fresh rosemary, fresh basil, and mozzarella. Toss to coat.
- Bake for 10 minutes, until bread is lightly browned.
- Remove from the oven and set aside.
- In a large dutch oven or soup pot, over medium-high heat, add 1 Tbsp. of olive oil, onion, and 3 garlic cloves. Saute for 5 minutes, until onions are translucent.
- Add in tomato paste, cook, stirring for 1 minute.
- Next add in all the tomatoes {minus ½ cup reserved for topping}, white beans, broth, 1 cup of water, rosemary sprig, red pepper flakes, and salt.
- Bring to a boil, reduce heat to medium for a simmer. Simmer for 20 minutes.
- Discard the rosemary sprig. Puree everything with an immersion blender. {if you don't have one then slowly add batches of the soup to a blender, puree and then return to the pot.
- Serve with croutons on top and a sprinkle of the freshly diced tomatoes. (JoyfulHealthyEats, Sept 2014)

Pesto Minestrone Soup:

Ingredients:

- 2 Tbsp. olive oil
- 1 large onion, finely chopped
- 2 celery sticks, finely chopped
- 1.4L vegetable stock
- 2 small lemons, zested and juiced
- 170g orzo
- 120g frozen peas
- 250g frozen spinach
- 50g pesto
- garlic flatbreads, to serve (optional)
- 60g parmesan (or vegetarian alternative), grated

Method:

- Heat the oil in a large saucepan, add the onion, celery, and a pinch of salt, and fry for 8 mins until soft. Add the stock with the zest and juice of the lemons, and season. Stir in the orzo and cook for 5 mins, then add the peas and spinach, and cook for a further 5 mins. Swirl through the pesto and season.
- Heat the flatbreads, if using, following pack instructions. Ladle the soup generously into bowls, and top with a handful of parmesan. Serve with the flatbread to dip. (Clark, Jan 2017)

Leek and Butter Bean Soup with Kale and Bacon:

Ingredients:

- 4 tsps. olive oil
- 500g leeks, sliced
- 4 thyme sprigs, leaves picked
- 2 x 400g cans butter beans
- 500ml vegetable bouillon stock
- 2 tsp. wholegrain mustard
- ½ small pack flat-leaf parsley
- 3 rashers streaky bacon
- 40g chopped kale, any tough stems removed
- 25g hazelnuts, roughly chopped

Method:

- Heat 3 tsps. oil in a large saucepan over a low heat. Add the leeks, thyme and seasoning. Cover and cook for 15 mins until softened, adding a splash of water if the leeks start to stick. Add the butter beans with the water from the cans, the stock and mustard. Bring to boil and simmer for 3-4 mins until hot. Blend the soup in a food processor or with a stick blender, stir through the parsley and check the seasoning by taste testing.
- Put the bacon in a large, non-stick frying pan over a medium heat. Cook for 3-4 mins until crispy, then set aside to cool. Add the remaining 1 tsp. oil to the pan, and tip in the kale and hazelnuts. Cook for 2 mins, stirring until the kale is wilted and crisping at the edges and the hazelnuts are toasted. Cut the bacon into small pieces, then stir into the kale mixture.
- Reheat the soup, adding a splash of water if it is too thick. Serve in bowls sprinkled with the bacon & kale mixture. (Gilhooly, Jan 2017)

Lentil and Butternut Squash Spiced Soup:

Ingredients:

- 2 Tbsp. olive oil
- 2 onions, finely chopped
- 2 garlic cloves, crushed
- ¼ tsp. hot chilli powder
- 1 Tbsp. ras el hanout
- 1 butternut squash, peeled and cut into 2cm pieces
- 100g red lentils
- 1L hot vegetable stock
- 1 small bunch coriander, leaves chopped, plus extra to serve
- dukkah (see tip) and natural yogurt, to serve

Method:

- Heat the oil in a large flameproof casserole dish or saucepan over a medium-high heat. Fry the onions with a pinch of salt for 7 mins, or until softened and just caramelized. Add the garlic, chilli, and ras el hanout and cook for 1 min more.
- Stir in the squash and lentils. Pour over the stock and season to taste. Bring to boil, then reduce the heat to a simmer and cook, covered, for 25 mins or until the squash is soft. Blitz the soup with a stick blender until smooth, then season to taste. To freeze, leave to cool completely and transfer to large freezer-proof bags.
- Stir in the coriander leaves and ladle the soup into bowls. Serve topped with the dukkah, yogurt and extra coriander leaves. (Clark, Sept 2019)

Creamy Cauliflower Soup:

Ingredients:

- 1 large cauliflower (1.5kg), cut into florets
- ½ Tbsp. ground cumin
- 2 Tbsp. olive oil, plus extra for drizzling
- 4 thyme sprigs
- 1 onion, finely chopped
- 1 celery stick, finely chopped
- 1 garlic clove, crushed
- 750-850ml veg or chicken stock
- 100ml single cream
- ½ small bunch of parsley, finely chopped

Method:

- Heat the oven to 390 degrees F. Toss the cauliflower florets in a roasting tin with 1 Tbsp. olive oil, the cumin and the thyme. Roast for 15 mins or until golden and tender. Discard the thyme.
- Heat the remaining oil in a saucepan with the onion and celery and fry over a medium heat for 10 mins or until softened. Add the garlic and cook for 1 min. Stir through most of the cauliflower, reserving some to top the soup with later. Add 750ml of the stock to the pan and bring to a simmer. Cook for 10 mins.
- Blitz the soup until smooth using a hand blender or food processor. Stir through the cream and season to taste. Add extra stock if you like your soup a little thinner. Ladle into bowls and top with the parsley, reserved cauliflower and an extra drizzle of olive oil. (Clark, Jan 2020)

Celeriac Root Soup:

Ingredients:

- 2 Tbsp. olive oil
- 300g celery, sliced, with tough strings removed
- 1 garlic clove, peeled
- 200g potatoes, peeled and cut into chunks
- 500ml vegetable stock
- 100ml milk
- crusty bread, to serve

Method:

- Heat the oil in a large saucepan over a medium heat, tip in the celery, garlic and potatoes and coat in the oil. Add a splash of water and a big pinch of salt and cook, stirring regularly for 15 mins, adding a little more water if the vegetables begins to stick.
- Pour in the vegetable stock and bring to boil, then turn the heat down and simmer for 20 mins further until the potatoes are falling apart and the celery is soft. Use a stick blender to purée the soup, then pour in the milk and blitz again. Season to taste. Serve with crusty bread. (Silcock, Dec 2017)

Broccoli and Pea Soup:

Ingredients:

- 1 Tbsp. rapeseed oil
- 1 onion, finely chopped
- 1 large garlic clove, crushed
- 400g broccoli, chopped into small florets
- 300g frozen peas
- 200g chard, chopped
- 1L low-salt vegetable stock
- ½ small bunch of basil, chopped
- small bunch of dill, chopped
- 1 lemon, zested and juiced
- 2 Tbsp. pumpkin seeds, toasted

Method:

- Heat the oil in a large saucepan. Add the onion and fry for 8 mins until soft and translucent. Add the garlic and cook for 1 min more. Tip in the broccoli, peas, and chard, then pour over the stock and bring the mixture to boil. Reduce the heat to a simmer, cover, and cook for 25 mins.
- Stir through the herbs, lemon zest, and juice, then blitz the soup with a stick blender until completely smooth. Ladle into bowls and serve with the toasted pumpkin seeds scattered over the top. (Clark, Sept 2019)

Supergreens Soup:

Ingredients:

- 2 tsps. olive oil
- 1 onion, chopped
- 2 garlic cloves, crushed
- 1 potato (approx 250g), cut into small cubes
- 600ml vegetable stock
- 120g bag mixed watercress, rocket and spinach salad
- 150g pot natural yogurt
- 20g pine nuts, toasted
- chilli oil, to serve (optional)

Method:

- Heat the oil in a medium saucepan over a low-medium heat. Add the onion and a pinch of salt, then cook slowly, stirring occasionally, for 10 mins until softened but not colored. Add the garlic and cook for 1 min more.
- Tip in the potato followed by the veg stock. Simmer for 10-12 mins until the potato is soft enough that a cutlery knife will slide in easily. Add the bag of salad and let it wilt for 1 min, then blitz the soup in a blender until it's completely smooth.
- Serve with a dollop of yogurt, some toasted pine nuts, and a drizzle of chilli oil, if you like. (Godwin, May 2016)

Chicken Broth Ramen with Salmon

Ramen is a popular dish all over the world. Just like the easy chicken soup, it is suitable for those colder months where you need some comfort but you don't want to go for something that is unhealthy. The Japanese flavors in this dish make it really exciting and interesting, and the healthy fats from the fish will serve in giving you lots of brainpower. Now that you know how easy it is to make bone broth, you can use it for the broth of this dish.

Ingredients:

- 1 piece chilimon, skin on
- 3 to 4 cups of chicken broth per serving
- 1 Tbsp. of fish paste
- 1 cup of rice noodles
- 1 bunch of preserved bamboo shoots
- 1 egg, boiled
- 1 stalk of green onions, chopped
- 1 Tbsp. of freshly chopped and peeled garlic
- 3 tsps. of soy sauce
- 1 bunch of snow peas
- 2 cloves of garlic
- 1 small chili, finely chopped and without seeds

Method:

- Mince the cloves of garlic and chop up the ginger, then fry them at a low temperature in a skillet until they are soft.
- Transfer the garlic and ginger and add the chicken broth to a saucepan and let simmer.
- Chop up the green onions and mushrooms from the top down.
- Line a baking sheet with parchment paper and put the salmon piece on top. Put in the oven to cook.

- While baking the salmon and simmering the stock, lightly fry the mushrooms in vegetable or sesame seed oil.
- Bring a medium-sized egg to hard-boil and deshell.
- Cook the ramen noodles, as indicated on the pack instructions.
- Serve by putting the cooked salmon into a bowl, then add the mushrooms and the stock. Top it with the green onions and the egg.

Fish Tacos

Fish tacos are a family favorite. You have a choice of using any whitefish that you like, and you can make the fish taco sauce healthy by using mostly natural yogurt mixed in with a small teaspoon of mayo. I have chosen cabbage, avocado, lime, and tomato as the toppings since these flavors go beautifully with the whitefish. This is a summer classic and one that will leave you thinking that you have gone out to one of your favorite restaurants! You can always substitute the fish with lean beef or chicken breast if you do not like fish.

Ingredients:

- whitefish: you may use cod, haddock, bass, or any other white fish you prefer
- whole wheat flour
- 2 tsps. of taco seasoning spices
- 1 tsp. of garlic powder
- A garnished amount of red cabbage, tomato, avocado, and lime for the toppings
- 1 tsp. of mayo with three Tbsps. of natural yogurt, mixed together
- corn flour tortillas

Method:

- Prep your fish by cutting it into one-inch cubes.
- Whisk together the flour, taco seasoning, garlic powder, cornstarch, salt, and pepper.
- Chop the avocado, red cabbage, tomatoes, and place them in a dish or bowl, while covering with a paper kitchen towel, as you prepare the rest.
- Whisk the yogurt, lime juice, taco seasoning, cayenne pepper, mayo, and black pepper together for the taco sauce.

- To cook the fish, dip the pieces into the flour mixture and pan fry for around 2 to 3 minutes on each side of a preheated skillet on a medium heat.
- Warm the tortillas in a cast iron skillet on high heat for around 10 seconds per side. Fill each tortilla with 3 or 4 pieces of fish, add the toppings and the sauce, and enjoy!

Refined Sugar Free Treats:

Chocolate Almond Cups:

Ingredients:

- 100g almonds, plus extra chopped almonds to serve
- ¼ cup (70g) almond or other nut butter
- ⅓ cup (65g) coconut oil, melted
- ¾ cup (50g) shredded coconut, plus extra to serve
- 2 Tbsp. rice malt syrup
- 1 tsp. ground cinnamon
- 1 tsp. vanilla extract
- 5 cups (100g) puffed rice
- ⅔ cup (160ml) maple syrup
- 140g coconut oil, melted, extra
- ⅔ cup (70g) cacao powder

Method:

- Grease holes of a 12-hole muffin pan and line with baking paper.
- Whiz almonds in a food processor until roughly chopped. Add nut butter, coconut oil, shredded coconut, rice malt syrup, cinnamon, vanilla and 2 Tbsps. maple syrup, and pulse to combine.
- Divide among holes of muffin pan, using a spoon to press down. Freeze for 10 minutes or until slightly firmed.
- Meanwhile, to make topping, combine extra coconut oil, cacao powder, and remaining ½ cup (125ml) maple syrup in a jug.
- Divide among muffin holes. Freeze for a further 30 minutes or until set. (Remove from pan and keep chilled if not serving immediately.)
- Top with extra almond and shredded coconut to serve. (Little, Feb 2017)

Sugar-Free Protein Clinkers:

Ingredients:

- 1 cup (100g) cacao powder, plus extra to coat
- 350g firm coconut oil
- 2 cups (500ml) rice malt syrup
- 500g desiccated coconut
- 100g vanilla protein powder
- 2 tsps. each finely grated beetroot and turmeric
- 50g raspberries, finely chopped
- finely grated zest and juice of 1 lemon
- 100g pistachios, finely chopped
- finely grated zest and juice of 1 lime
- 1 vanilla bean, split, seeds scraped

Method:

- To make the glaze, place cacao, 200g oil, and 160ml rice malt syrup in a saucepan over low heat and cook, stirring until smooth and combined. Set aside.
- To make fillings, whiz coconut, protein powder, ¼ cup (60ml) hot water, and remaining 150g oil and 340ml rice malt syrup in a food processor. Divide evenly among 4 bowls.
- Add beetroot and berry to 1 bowl; turmeric, lemon zest and juice to the second; pistachios, lime zest and juice to the third; and vanilla seeds to the last. Stir each to combine. With wet hands, roll 1 Tbsp mixture into a ball and place on a tray. Repeat with remaining mixture. Freeze for 30 minutes or until firm. (Coutts, Oct 2017)

Sugar-free Chocolate and Sticky Date Pudding:

Ingredients:

- 375g fresh medjool dates, pitted
- 150g buckwheat flour
- 3 cups (300g) almond meal
- ⅓ cup (35g) raw cacao powder
- 1 vanilla bean, split, seeds scraped (reserve pod for another use)
- 1 ½ tsp. bicarbonate of soda
- 225g solidified coconut oil
- 150g sugar-free dark chocolate (from supermarkets and health food stores), finely chopped
- 6 eggs, lightly beaten
- 300ml buttermilk

Warm Vanilla Coconut Sauce:

- 800ml coconut milk
- 200g fresh medjool dates, pitted
- 2 vanilla beans, split, seeds scraped

Method:

- Place dates in a bowl and cover with 3 cups (750ml) boiling water. Stand for 10 minutes to soften, then drain and finely chop.
- To make the pudding, place chopped dates and remaining ingredients in a bowl and stir to combine.
- Spread batter into prepared dish, smoothing the surface with a palette knife, and bake for 50 minutes to 1 hour or until a skewer inserted in pudding comes out clean.
- Meanwhile, for the warm vanilla and coconut sauce, combine all ingredients in a saucepan over high heat and bring to a simmer. Remove from heat, transfer to a blender and whiz until smooth. Set aside for 10 minutes to infuse.
- Remove pudding from the oven and, using a skewer, poke holes from the top through to the bottom. Pour one-third of the sauce over the hot pudding and stand for 5 minutes or until the sauce is absorbed slightly.
- Serve warm with remaining sauce. (Duggan, July 2017)

Rawmisu:

Ingredients:

- 150g pitted prunes, roughly chopped
- ¼ cup (60ml) Marsala or fortified wine
- ½ cup (125ml) espresso
- 2 Tbsp. cacao, plus extra to dust
- 1 Tbsp. freshly ground coffee
- ⅓ cup (80ml) rice malt syrup, melted
- ½ cup (80g) white chia seeds
- 400ml can coconut milk
- 2 tsps. vanilla extract
- ⅓ cup (40g) cacao nibs

Method:

- Soak prunes in Marsala (or substitute water) and espresso. Set aside for 3 hours.
- Meanwhile, combine cacao, ground coffee, 2 Tbsp rice malt syrup, ¼ cup (40g) chia seeds, 150ml coconut milk and ¾ cup (185ml) warm water in a bowl. Stir to combine well, then transfer to an airtight container and chill for 3 hours.
- Place vanilla and remaining ¼ cup (40g) chia seeds, 2 Tbsp. rice malt syrup and 250ml coconut milk in a separate bowl and stir to combine well, then transfer to an airtight container and chill for 3 hours.
- To serve, beat the vanilla and chocolate chia mousses with a spoon to soften. Spoon prunes into 4 serving glasses. Top with half the vanilla chia mousse, then top with chocolate chia mousse, then finish with a final layer of vanilla chia mousse. Sprinkle with extra cacao and scatter with cacao nibs. (Harley, Oct 2015)

Honey and Lemon Curd Tart with Blueberries:

Ingredients:

- 375g block frozen puff pastry, thawed
- 2 x 125g punnets blueberries
- micro coriander, to serve (optional)

Honey and Lemon Curd:

- 6 eggs
- juice of 2 lemons, zest finely grated
- ⅓ cup (115g) honey, plus extra to serve
- 1 cup (250ml) coconut oil, melted

Method:

- For the lemon curd, place all ingredients in a saucepan over low heat, whisking for 2-3 minutes until thickened. Set aside to cool. Chill for 1-2 hours to thicken further.
- Roll out the pastry to a 15cm x 30cm rectangle. Place on a baking paper-lined baking tray and prick all over with a fork. Cover with another sheet of baking paper and another baking tray, then bake at 180C for 15 minutes or until crisp and golden. Cool.
- Spread pastry with curd and scatter over blueberries. Drizzle with extra honey and sprinkle with micro coriander, if using, to serve.

Conclusion

Thank you very much for reading *Gastric Band Hypnosis for Rapid Weight Loss*! In this book, you've read about how excess weight affects millions of people and how many intricacies there are at work behind that issue. We have covered the different things that can help you to solve all the problems of excess weight, and we've introduced some new ways of thinking about the difficulties that can arise when you're trying to live the healthiest lifestyle possible.

Weight loss without proper nutrition simply isn't sustainable and, in the cases of so many crash diets, it can even be damaging to your body, your mental state, and your metabolism. Proper nutrition, adequate and vigorous physical activity are absolutely crucial to the weight loss journey, particularly one that results in sustained and healthy weight loss. Many people who have experienced a monumental weight loss only to gain it back within a couple of years have reported that their weight gain resumed when they went back to their normal eating habits after their weight goal was reached. It's only in the event of true lifestyle change that weight loss can really be sustainable.

For some, weight loss simply isn't achievable by traditional or "normal" means thanks to subconscious blocks, physical limitations, genetic specificities, health anomalies, and more. In such cases, or even in cases where you simply need a little bit of extra strength and help, it seems that addressing the subconscious is the real answer. The subconscious can hold the key to a vast array of troubles that we may never even be consciously aware of.

It turns out that self-hypnosis can allow you to be your own guide and to put the future of your own weight loss in your hands. Self-hypnosis allows you to choose the phrases that you want your subconscious to be giving back to you in those situations. When your conscious mind thinks "weight loss," your subconscious mind may think "I'm behind," or "I need to do better." With self-hypnosis, however, you can take control and put a new response in your subconscious. When your conscious mind thinks weight loss moving forward, your subconscious mind could think, "weight loss comes so easily to me," or something equally as revolutionary to your weight loss thought process.

That healthy thought process, it turns out, has a lot to do with your weight loss success. When your subconscious mind is constantly throwing negative phrases at you in response to your conscious thoughts regarding your goals, you might not feel like they're quite attainable or feasible. However, if you're telling your subconscious mind that they are attainable, that you are capable of attaining them, and that you are *worthy* of them, then your subconscious mind will feed all that positivity right back to you as a matter of course.

Your next step in your weight loss journey and your weight loss success is to get started with your self-hypnosis right now! Use the information in this book to your advantage and create the life that, on a subconscious level, you've been telling yourself that you cannot have!

Grab life by the reins and get a move on!

If you want to get the Free Audio version of the book, scan this QR Code

Thank you for reading This book!

If you enjoyed it, please visit the site where your purchased it and write a brief review.

Your feedback is important to me and will help other readers decide whether to read the book too.

Printed in Great Britain
by Amazon

84355377R00153